P9-CRU-300

Cherishing Sophia

Rising to Authenticity and Feminine Power

Copyright © 2007 Julie K. Lynch
All rights reserved. No part of this book may be reproduced in any form or by any electronic or mechanical means including information storage and retrieval systems without permission in writing from the author except where permission is noted within the book for personal use or except by a reviewer who may quote brief passages in a review.

First Printing

Sunray Publishing
25123 22nd Avenue
St. Cloud, MN 56301

Manufactured in the United States of America

ISBN-10: 0-9785081-7-3
ISBN-13: 978-0-9785081-7-3

New Revised Standard Version Bible, copyright 1989, Division of Christian Education of the National Council of the Churches of Christ in the United States of America. Used by permission. All rights reserved.

Cherishing Sophia

Rising to Authenticity and Feminine Power

Julie K. Lynch

edited by

Stefanie Weisgram, O.S.B.

Joanna Pucell, Associate Professor
Communication Studies
St. Cloud State University

Table of Contents

Dedication

To Pat, Sean, and Cody: the roses showering my life with delicate love and tears of joy.

To women who dare know authentic form, and to men who dare understand.

Introduction:

Breathe

I'm savoring the experience of writing for women and bringing them to joy. May this book caress you and touch something deep within you. May this book carry you and comfort you. May my words transform something of your being and your growing edges.

When I run, I am momentarily complete. During thirty minutes I move into timelessness and freedom. My body struggles near the beginning, feels the effort in various locations of my being, and adjusts to the challenge. I divert myself with thoughts of the day, psyching up for the roles I'll play and the schedule I need to maintain. Then my thoughts begin to wander and move into deeper levels of sensing where I need, emotionally, to go. I liken these thoughts to the rhythm just before slumber: rational to irrational; sensing to senseless; complete, to incomplete. Almost assuredly, my body falls into a robotic pumping rhythm with its unthinking routine of stepping, pacing, moving, and completing. My body and mind seem one and separate in this same experience. The culmination of endorphins being released, body coming into its own, and mental moving into spiritual being allows me to feel such calm, strength, and vision of who I am in this day and in this life. Frequently I notice something about my Self, my relationships, or my work that moves me into a new perception and awareness. My mind parallels this rhythm and I sense the wonderment of that which is my life.

My noticings, perceptions, and awareness fueled me to create a vision for other women who are in need of something more … a perception switch. I intuit the need, and it presented itself in research as I read a college survey a few years back. It affirmed the truth I saw: college men *over*estimate their intelligence, and college women *under*estimate their intelligence. I am appalled at the incongruity and I see this perceived reality in my own classroom. Women I admire as strong achievers are questioning the quality of their work. Women can be this far from the objective truth of their capability and talent? I am frustrated that I can teach excellence in presenting self to others, while women remain inwardly uncomfortable with image of self. I see the missing piece – *the work of being excellent comes from within and without.* Believing within births a byproduct far beyond confidence – a countenance … a power derived from wisdom and intuitive connection to truth and spirit. This book was birthed in those moments of frustration when I stopped and took note of what women deserve. I teach and write to encourage *countenance of being*, rather than confidence of doing. The result is authorship and ownership of True Self.

Women who reach mid-life without inner connection struggle. Past, shallow coping mechanisms were created, but no longer serve. The fun of socializing and partying evolves into health problems and/or addictions as women wonder where the fun has gone. Further, our entire culture is suffering: fatigue, over-stimulation, and a sense life is moving much too fast as dreams are fading. A boatride on the river allowed me to hear sadness as a woman spoke of her writing gift never realized. A friend continues to submit to a controlling partner as if she has no choice. A friend laments her son's choice to go fight in Iraq. Another fights to keep her husband, family, and sense of Self intact as dis-ease and financial threat become a reality. Women lament wishes lost believing perceptions of limitation. Perceptions turn into created realities of being stuck, helpless, and unable to find opportunity for happiness, love, and calm. I cannot change life circumstance, but I can present women with invigorating, endless opportunities of hope and energy brought forth from inner understanding and calm. Intuitive knowing brings a sense of light and wisdom to come through life's journey as creatures of wondrous beauty. Life is fun again.

Intuitive wisdom cannot be measured. It's timeless and ageless. Engaging with a path created to find life's brilliance is an ageless task and an ongoing task. Allow my words to remind you of what you already know but are not remembering to see. Allow a vision of a unique woman arising walking a new path derived from changed perception blended with invigorating energy from within that bursts through and lavishes a surrounding world.

I Dare Live Without Limitation.

I teach with every fiber of my being, quite naturally. The "what" I want others to learn about perception and communication is shifting dramatically: the "what" is now an awakening to true form and place. My research expertise is created with frameworks and structures of communication and psychology and recent knowledge gained from attending and presenting at the national level. Currently, I'm presenting in the area of contemplative listening. Dr. Maria Roca, Florida Gulf Coast University, and I lead discussion and planning for the next five years of research in this area. Results will be communicated nationally and internationally through the International Listening Association; however, the research will truly arrive as meaningful when it is applied to the real-life experiences of students and the truth of their holistic development.

Students invigorate my need to derive meaning and create meaningful application of research. I rely on a vast background in educational theory: Gardner's Multiple Intelligences guide my words to speak to different learning styles; and Bloom's Taxonomy inspires me to provide audience with content, yet to guide into deeper, integrated learning through experiences of knowing. I am a teacher by nature, a vessel of knowledge and experience searching to create connection each and every time we examine communicative, psychological, and contemplative excellence in light of our perceptions of truth and reality as we continue to know ourselves as growing, dynamic instrumental beings. Students fill me with energy and inspire me to continue learning and giving.

An Invitation to Become Someone More

Open up to create an image of a message created especially and, perhaps, divinely for you alone to hear. Write the mental list you need to come into being. Women who read this book are ready for a perception switch … they are literal and figurative movers and shakers searching within to find depth of who they are and who they are meant to be. Movers and shakers will create new perceptions desperately needed in our culture toward healing, acceptance, and celebration. Indeed, celebrate gratitude of knowing the giftedness of opportunity to grow into a woman who cherishes and is cherished – breath by breath.

I love epiphanies. I always have. The "aha" of noticing something, rather enormous or small has always been the path to the next place in my life. I'm viewed as impulsive, but there's always a point at which I can remember deciding to move into the intuitive piece and to trust. I assure you I'm as rational as the rest of our culture; although in a culture where most make decisions based on priorities of money, time and getting ahead, I seem rather out of the ordinary. To my intuitive Self or center I make complete sense and trust the next step of my journey. The "ahas" create a stunning way for us all to dance through life. We are all nudged to notice and embrace who we *authentically are* in this life. Those who don't listen to spirit have not fully moved into the strength, confidence, and empowerment of their authentic, grand being. I wish you "ahas'" and epiphanies and dancing.

Running is a metaphor of our life's circular journey. We spiral through the challenges and suffering, moving into the rhythm of what these pains can teach us, finally reaching the rhythm of what is meant uniquely for us to know and experience. The understanding of our experiences allows us to look at our life patterns and see the pieces that have fallen into place exactly as they should for our true being. The people we've met, connected with, fought with, and suffered with become the thread weaving the pieces of understanding of what we truly want in life and what we truly do not want in life. Our panorama of life experience is the snapshot moment setting the stage for the future journey of living beautifully and powerfully.

Owning and naming one's power begins with developing self-confidence and removing negative thought. When I teach public speaking I witness people come into their own in such a visual manner. Teaching is, in fact, an incredibly rich and spiritual experience. I am the catalyst, and they learn how to embrace what they already possess. Watching an individual learn to trust him/her Self and intuit his/her own remarkable gifts after focusing nervous energy and removing self-doubt is immensely rewarding. Owning one's strength and confidence is a beautiful parallel for moving deeper into Spiritual Self. Body is the vessel and we learn how to embrace the spirit or breath we possess. We author countenance.

The harmony of balancing positive and negative emotions or tensions commences with breathing. When public speaking students feel fear their breathing is choppy and ineffective, allowing the blood to pulse to the emotional station of the brain. The lack of cognitive thinking causes physical feelings of lightheadedness and weakness – yet the emotional override can be halted. Students learn to control fear with a simple pause. Students derive the perception of being "okay" or "on" in performance from a simple, complete breath properly filling the diaphragm and releasing tension with a slow, steady miracle of release--a pause. Life takes us into moments of rushed breathing when emotions control and brains try to keep up. A simple breath can bring us back to the performance of our reality. A pause in life gives us the glimpse of our quiet power.

Pausing and Mindfulness

When we pause we become fully present to the moment. A fully present moment presents our inner spirit or intuitive guidance. We capture clarity and awareness in an instant. *Spirit* is actually derived from the word *espiritu* that means *breath*. Every *body* has a spirit. Words limit because spirituality is such a profound essence of pure joy in our experience when we learn to walk through life in something different from logical or rational perspective. Spirituality is what magnificently touches us in our hearts and intuitive place. Ronald Rolheiser, in his book *Holy Longing*, explains that the freedom of choice is in our focused passion. Rolheiser says, "What we do with that fire, how we channel it, is our spirituality." Opening up to a multitude of spiritual opportunities guides us into being truly awakened to the passion of our existence. I find baking a strawberry-rhubarb pie while listening to Joni Mitchell an incredibly rich spiritual experience. Some prefer a walk in the woods, others meditate and/or learn yoga, others pray. William James wrote about the revelation of our spiritual experiences. He concludes:

> ***It is as if there were in the human consciousness a sense of reality, a feeling of objective presence, a perception of what we may call 'something there,' more deep and more general than any of the special and particular 'senses' by which the current psychology supposes existent realities to be originally revealed."***
>
> – William James, *The Varieties of Religious Experience*

Our spiritual "voice" is the place of power deep within that can take us outward toward miraculous experiences. It's created and creative. Our created/creative centers can't be wrong either.

Unlike measurable outcomes of career path and worldly successes, spiritual journey cannot be measured or compared. We can't do a spiritual journey wrong. It lovingly is whatever *it is.* Spirituality is as preciously unique as our created beings and all spirits deserve to be authentically beheld.

Barriers to Mindfulness

Our perceptions teach us to be busy and to hate being alone. Ultimate joy is reached when we journey to the core of our essence and even learn to embrace our aloneness. Henry Nouwen, an author who writes of the spirituality of life states, "By attentive living we can learn the difference between being present in loneliness and being present in solitude." Are we afraid to be alone because that is when we sense our broken spirit? Our inner child is calling us to come back into purity and the play of celebrating life. Solitude presents us with opportunity to do so.

Our culture thinks and analyzes too much. It's dissonant to our well-being. Our culture perceives fear when something is beyond rational thinking. We want to explain, we want to control. Control is only a mask for broken spirit, and it's time to stop the deception of believing we need control. In the deception of control, we can disguise our fear that we are longing to feel like we fit in. Our intuitive self is shouting for us to awaken and admit to fears of loneliness, disconnection and wanting so desperately for more. We intuitively sense what we spend our lives coming to … a revelation or "aha" moment of knowing what spiritual writer Thomas Merton describes as:

> ***an insatiable longing for beauty and harmony, a painful aching to experience life as we sense it might be: fulsome and delightful in its symmetry and grace***
>
> – Thomas Merton, *The Wisdom of the Desert.*

Society teaches us to disguise with our busyness and we further distance ourselves from our spirit, joy, love, and compassion.

"Ahas' reveal themselves in the silence of my breath when I am alone. My heart tells me I've intentionally been given the pieces I need for this writing that move me from my solitude into connection with women who want more and deserve more. I take the clay of my spirit and shape my "ahas" into words and visions of feminine and masculine power as you pause to share with me in this brief, but vital journey toward beauty and dignity. I breathe the whisper of truth as I hope all women may dance toward authenticity, connectedness, and joy.

As we dance, we choose the unique path of our spirit. We choose love and we choose joy. Breathing voraciously through life fills every fiber of our very being with our fire. Centered, we know to *just be* in our passion. *Just being* opens our senses to pleasure and beauty and the deepest knowing. We move ahead with strength rather than weakness, creating connection to others' spirits and passion derived from the deepest knowing in our daily quietude.

We breathe. We focus on the present moment. We gift ourselves with a pleasant inhale of cool air and a deep exhale allowing us to let go of the stress and to remember our energy, our passion. Our heart's passion speaks of what we really need. When we fill ourselves with a cleansing breath while listening to the essence of what we need, we are caring for ourselves and paying attention to ourselves. What do *we need*?

We spend a lot of time being rational, being in our heads. Frequently we are out of balance. We limit passionate experiences that are our motivation to change thoughts, perceptions, attitudes, values and beliefs on divine truth. During persuasion, someone paints a picture of his/her truth and we see it, we get it. We feel a new perception in our hearts and then go back up into our heads to justify it, and we do this so quickly and naturally that we barely notice the process. Aristotle used the term *logos* for logic and facts (head) and *pathos* for passionate appeals (heart). Truth needs both. He knew humans were heart and head. Spirit connects heart and head and names our needs.

Ask for the World

Logic is not enough. It is limited. Alone, science and head limit. The head is where limitations and barriers exist due to our perceptions. In our intuitive hearts, we feel all is possible. In our intuitive hearts we can ask for the world if we are open. We return to our heads with thoughts and visions of love shaped by our heart. The heartfelt visions walk with our rational visions anew with possibility. Our visions, our spirituality, are powerfully **pro**active rather than **re**active. We create hope and change when we heal our broken spirit.

Spirituality, for many, is a meaningful personal relationship with the energy of our world, God, or Supreme Being. There's a profound, exquisite tenderness and unconditional love waiting within. Unconditional love is our healing of broken spirit and we return to creating the exquisite intentions of our lives. Some choose to channel spirituality into beautiful works of art, literature, music, or kindness to others. It's impossible to create beauty with a broken spirit – an intuited pain. Creativity **is** wholeness.

My head and my heart are guiding the writing of this book. My ego is rational and necessary, but also removed as I go deeper to an intuitive knowing. Writing from my heart, my listening, my compassion allows me to connect with women. Imagine when it is dusk – between light and dark, rational and beyond rational. One magnificent star flickers like the countenance of one woman's spirit. Soon, more stars shine their brilliance and we see the connected beauty of the constellations and the luminosity of the night sky. Women are in need of something far greater than what our culture tells us is success. Women need the countenance of their light. Women need to reconnect and heal from their sufferings so they can shine.

Birthing this book means I've done what I can to actively help women in their journey toward complete joy. In fact, I've spent the last four years immersed in a rigorous spiritual program at The Saint Benedict Monastery. I learned **all is possible.** I learned joy. I learned to move out of my head and into my heart. It's all about removing the barriers and daring to become what we are intended to be. I want to take my precious experience to all women in the form of this writing. Something will resonate with your life experience thus allowing you to be nudged in some manner. And when we are nudged and touched, we feel valued and loved and connected amid the noise and busyness of this world. May you allow the touching of your growing edge to complete you. May you open up toward a whole new experience of living, loving, and receiving. I am writing *for* you. I *value* you.

Ask for the World … To Have Peace.

We have the ability to resolve conflict and achieve peace with self, others, and even on a global scale. We can no longer "fight for peace". Rather, we remember the power of inner calm and truth to provide the path of hope, peace, and harmony in our world. Ironically, even religions presently divide, though they are capable of new perceptions contributing to world peace. Rather than view religions in terms of their differences, we can rise to knowing similarities of unconditional love and acceptance of the other and perceptions of goodness. The Dalai Lama said, "The world's religions can contribute to world peace, if there is peace and growing harmony between different faiths." It is through reverence and respect that our world will transcend its violence. It begins with one woman's spiritual brilliance flickering and connecting in the night sky. Her spirit flickers in her breath. Some women meditate, Some women pray. We all breathe, we all have spirit, we all love and are loved and take that out to others with our voice.

Breathe again. Feel yourself fill up with the energy of oxygen and the passion of life. Carl Jung once said, "I simply believe that some part of the human Self … is not subject to the laws of time and space." When we are able to feel our breath and our spirit, we are able to let go of limitation and evoke our passion. We recognize and *know* authentic Self and limitless being. I applaud all women who have the gift of their truth. Imagine the glorious people they're to become. A transcendent view of our experience is calling to be acknowledged rather than ignored. Women in their quietude know "this is not enough." Women cannot settle for shallow existences and relationships. Women must *know* the depth we can fathom. Women must get beyond rational perspective to sense or feel beyond rational existence. Our sensuality and truth allow us to move in a mystical way – a way of living where we are swallowed by life and mystery and graced by the pleasure of it all. What if everything is possible? What if we can ask for the world?

Live Your Best Life

When she walks into the room,
everybody turns:

some kind of light is coming from her head.
Even the geraniums look curious …
We're all attracted to the perfume
of fermenting joy.

we've all tried to start a fire,
and one day maybe it will blaze up on its own.
In the meantime, she is the one today among us
most able to bear the idea of her own beauty,
and when we see it, what we do is natural:

we take our burned hands
out of our pockets,
and clap.
– Tony Hoagland, *Grammar*

Listen to your breaths, your voice, your center. Our desire to "get there" as we connect with spirit welcomes us with gifts of love and compassion and power. We live intentionally, with freedom and times of joy and exhilaration. Our journey is not about running away from something, or running ahead to get to something … we simply learn to enjoy the run.

Chapter One

Beholding Beauty, Sharing Secrets, and Best Friends

Don't worry about the future, or worry, but know that worrying is as effective as trying to solve an algebra equation by chewing bubblegum. The real troubles in your life are apt to be things that never crossed your worried mind; the kind that blindside you at 4pm on some idle Tuesday. Do one thing every day that scares you.
– Baz Luhrman, *Sunscreen Song*

We're standing at a crossroads, an intersection of gravel and tar. The tar represents the easy manner with which we can easily sail through life unaffected by our surroundings, yet still arriving to an unknown destination. The gravel represents a choice of slowing down, of being aware of our surroundings ... the loose rock, the curving around apple trees, corn fields, creeks and bridges showing the prevalance of natural beauty and provision of everything we need. We either choose the ease traveling through life quite unaffected, yet complacently achieving – or we become incredibly and undeniably aware of our inner need to gather so much more from life. We thrive in awareness, being affected and affecting others, and deeply knowing we are authentically *making life happen* rather than allowing it to *happen to us*. We are created beings with power to enjoy the ride of our lives; the ultimate fun and joy and laughter of our existence.

First, we must resolve the conflict we've created with our narratives of inner self. We create the illusion we are stuck or paralyzed, narratives of inner turmoil, conflict, and limitation. We are against our Selves each time we sense dissonance and do not unpack and sort until we discover truth. We let go of the limitation and evoke our inner freedom. My tongue is white and dry and parched from swallowing dust, though it is not the dust of the gravel path. Indeed, it is the dust of denying my most profound existence. I swallow and gulp and compromise to please distorted, chaotic societies while I note dissonance. The dust is dissipated passion. I learned to speak authentically and quench my thirst rather than swallow integrity and remain parched. A soul's voice intuits authentic beauty of being in just the right place and doing just the right choices in life – as if we are *remembering*. We feel "at home" in moments such as this. We make life happen when we mindfully notice and drink to our clarity of choice. We create a space to see our choices and evoke our freedom. We continue to resolve our inner conflict throughout life, and maintain our liberation.

I'm a *beholder*. I've created the term because I see too many people wasting their intense energy and passion into negative emotions of worry, stress, and anger. A necessary change in our world needs to take place with connection, love and compassion as all women *behold* their true strength and potential – which is also their beauty. I'm searching for a label that works for this vision. Women's liberation in the sixties liberated quite a lot of submissive roles and moved women forward in great strides – but the label is dated and carries bra-burning connotations. Incidentally, it bears noting the bra-burning incident never actually occurred and was created by the media, but that's another issue in another book. Liberation to move into knowing and loving one's self is a freeing and appealing idea, but perhaps we are still stopping a bit short of what women deserve. The label of "feminist" is admirable in many arenas. Feminists change policies, laws and environments toward equality and nurtured health. I admire the many opportunities they've won and continued to fight for as we win what always should have been. Unfortunately, the label "feminist" connotes less than desirable meaning, due to anti-male messages, affecting perception of the listener in negative rather than empowered manner.

Further, our culture speaks messages of glass ceilings and limitation – forgetting we can shatter these same images. I speak from an intuitive sense of limitless potential – a means of living fully awakened to reality, yet empowered by inner knowing of so much more possibility. It's a relief from the repeated messages students hear--of what women cannot do. I'm a rebel. I *behold* each woman in her beauty and refuse to listen to the "cannots". "Cannots" are nothing more than wasted energy. "Cannots" are no fun. We deserve the fun of dancing through our lives in magnificent form. Each woman can and will open up to her truest potential if she is inspired to do so.

When I was an undergraduate, I admired Joan Baez. I loved her music, but my connection to her stirred from a space more profound than mere admiration. She embodied my definition of happiness: heartfelt giving in romantic relationship and heartfelt giving through created social change. Joan named a voice of inner beauty transformed into loving extension. Her political activism named truth when a culture was unfocused and dissipated in chaos. While establishments trusted boundaries, limits and rules and a government that no longer protected, she remembered who she was and led us to a higher consciousness of who we were. Joan's soul created narratives of romance, truth, and hope for social change to rise above media messages of hopelessness and confusion. She birthed authenticity and wisdom. Most importantly, Joan created a culture of unity from her wholeness. Her music represented harmony--not dissonance. Joan Baez sang until *herstory* became *history*.

Wholeness evokes unity. Dissonant feminists who move into masculine power also bring authority and change – but sometimes *at the expense of* feminine power of cooperation and connectedness. Feminists who remain in anger and speak against males are choosing to do so. They are stuck and cannot embrace both genders or be effective with others. These women are so passionate about the social justice of gender equality they actually move into a negative perception of males, creating division rather than wholeness. Some men deserve anger and restitution for their actions; however, divided energy also removes focus on the goal with connection, compassion, and love – our true feminine power. Additionally, the "worry" applied to males often removes or distracts true focus of what women can be about toward major change. Noticeably, women who become anti-male create negative energy of distrust, anger, and victimization. Women who busy themselves in the negativity not only lose focus, but give power to males who keep women too busy in this arena to remain focused and moving forward toward goals – it is, conceivably, a tactic in many instances. The negativity disperses and divides focus, literally lessening intense feminine power as the fire of channeling toward goals moves into smaller flames, then sparks too exhausted to remain afire. The existence of this distraction has even moved into our language. Students frequently discuss those who are "male-bashers", giving the term feminist a negative connotation. I'm certainly not a "male-basher". A perception of deserved equality easily shifts into inappropriate boundaries of "getting even". Anger divides. We cannot waste our power in division of women and men. Division is a perception of reality that needn't be our truth. Both genders win when we move into understanding and connection rather than competition and comparing. We achieve wholeness when genders embrace feminine connectedness and masculine authority. Our truth embraces both women and men. Connectedness creates our power, our authority of being.

Our connectedness becomes our outer authority of power, our masculine side. Becoming our truth in connection results in an automatic countenance of true confidence, wisdom, growth. We find our Self, our identity, our truth, our focused channel. Further, we connect with men and women as we show them our power. Our true energy and passion is always positive in nature. I am a beholder who looks to help all women know deeply about their beauty. I want women to resonate with each other's respect and support and knowing of beauty in diversified ways. Our beauty is birthed with love and compassion and positive emotion … and fun. As beholders we look to bring others (women and men) to the truth of their existence. We see our own beauty with such clarity and playfully remember the passion of our existence.

What follows is a virtual tour of your deepest value and wisdom. The warmth of our souls radiating remembrance illuminates the familiar path we followed as children of fun, play, worth, and authentic intent. Life created the barriers – the virtual tour will gently remove the walls we thought we needed, but which served only to limit. We lift brick by brick and release the familiar interior freedom of our treasured giftedness. We open up to a view of our wildest desires and dreams.

Perceived Self

A pink Begonia was once given to me as a token of appreciation for my teaching at a university. I planted the pink flower in my herb garden to remind me daily through the summer of the affirmation of my self-worth and self-love. I was already deeply touched with the success of the semester and the flower simply affirmed I was in the right place. I just arrived from an opposite place where I had burned myself out trying to prove I was "good enough". I was losing inner conflict and drowning in dissonance. Teaching in a spiritual environment, at St. John's University, reminded me of harmony: I was "good enough". What a relief to channel my energy into excellence rather than fear! Wow. Let me be very clear: I didn't change myself at either establishment, the *perception of me* changed, because I resolved my inner conflict. Others saw me in strength, not weakness. If we are trying to be good, ethical people, we need to remember true perception of *knowing* "good enough"--especially when others aren't seeing it. When we see our goodness, we know our harmony. We confront ourselves face-to-face in solitude and evoke what is needed for our healthy growth and self-talk. The first brick we lift is artificial perception. Inner spirit perceptions are pure.

Perceptions begin when we are children and have no knowledge of how to explain our world or our place in it. Children look to others and allow the reflection to create self-concept. In 1902, C.H. Cooley, a U.S. sociologist, claimed we perceive our inner self each time we view another's image of us in communication. His couplet explains:

> ***Each to each a looking glass***
> ***Reflects the other that doth pass.***

Further, Cooley states our assessment of self in relationship with others is divided into three principle elements:

1. the imagination of our appearance to the other person
2. the imagination of his [her] judgement of that appearance
3. Some sort of self-feeling, such as pride or mortification.

For example, in my childhood I was highly creative and praised for performance. When I was a little girl, I crossed my legs on my Aunt Bev's avocado green couch and sucked in my nostrils. I licked my upper lip with the tip of my tongue and played with the skirt of my dress as I rocked forward and backward imitating Lily Tomlin's character of Edith Ann from the television show, *Rowan and Martin's Laugh-in*. I could make my parents, grandparents, and cousins laugh. I continue to want others to laugh, to lighten up, to have fun in life. Conversely, a woman once made a face at me, and I knew she was making fun of me because I had big eyes. Which perception served my well-being? We remember to sort out and let go of memories that don't serve our true, created being. We molded our inner beings into our own paper mache layering of newspaper strip experiences. Each layer reinforces or introduces new stories from perceptions of others and we have gift of changing self-perception and ridding ourselves of artificial perception throughout life – if we dare choose to do the work of change.

Even as adults, we constantly check mirrors for reassurance we are okay: as if the literal and figurative mirrors provide the clarity of defining acceptance. It bears noting a perception difference: males try to fix any external flaws, while females internalize the external flaws. Wow – such a signifcant difference! We re-wet the newspaper strips with fresh glue and apply only loving messages to internal self and create paper mache of acceptance and unconditional love. Inside us lies an inner child of ego still wanting to be perceived as "okay".

Beliefs are our created perceptions, and we hold them in our power. We choose the perceptions. Our very freedom lies in our power to choose perceptions of value. We pause and become mindful of our childhood. We view, fully present, what our childhood was like. A few weeks ago, I was seated next to a very dear girl with big brown eyes who showed me her bright pink bubble gum. Her mother explained this was her first time getting gum, so I praised her ability to chew gum. It wasn't long before she showed me she could also pray. She folded her hands so carefully and struggled with crossing her two index fingers. She bowed her head so low her chin was pushed into the red velvet of her dress. The endearing image produced many positive verbal messages from her mother and from me. Children who are told positive messages create positive perceptions or stories about their being. They are "so cute" and "smart" and "such a good girl". The same girl could be in a dynamic or environment where she does not receive complimentary messages. Would that mean the little girl is no longer good? Of course not! And her soul *knows* her goodness either way – but the environment either supports what her soul knows or creates messages of dissonance – and she has power through life to accept or reject those messages, to find her own harmony. Unfortunately, children raised in more difficult environments receive the opposite messages and begin to believe they are "no good" or "stupid" or "too much trouble". Awhile ago my family attended a fundraiser allowing families to come into an art studio and create bowls of pottery that would be used to feed the poor. My husband and I helped our children create bowls. Pottery-making is a very relaxing experience, but it is also far more difficult than it first appears. A young girl was struggling with her clay. She had formed it and was spinning it, but the wheel took on more speed than her small hands could handle as she wetted the brown clay. The result was a collapsed side. Her mother remarked, "You're just not good at being creative." Consider the potential message of that statement. It would be possible for the young girl to walk her life for a great amount of time with the story of believing she could not be creative. In effect, she would virtually choose her very decisions on creative opportunities accordingly if she believed in the story, thus denying herself the very pleasure of creative development and beauty. My dear friend was told this same message – and she is now a fabulous writer – thank goodness she chose not to believe a reality of limitation.

When I was a young girl, my parents never mentioned my getting married. I was always told I would attend college. Perceptions were different in the eighties, and women in small towns of central Minnesota didn't yet believe they could choose to remain single. Somehow, I perceived this to mean I wasn't "good enough" to get married. Another perception added to this story when I visited my grandmother's house. When I was very young, I played with two cousins similar in age quite frequently. We three girls became close friends and even sometimes received similar Christmas gifts. One Christmas our grandparents gave each of my two cousins beautiful bride dolls encased in plastic for safekeeping. I received the only bridesmaid doll! I thought she was quite beautiful and cherished her for years – but each Saturday morning I dusted her as she added into the story I created, that I would not get married, I would go to college. In my perception, I would not be able to choose to marry.

As an adult, I know my parents lovingly meant for me to choose marriage or not choose marriage, and they proudly envisioned my college career. In fact, of twenty-four cousins, I was the first one who attended college. *I* chose the distorted reality – and they weren't even aware of or responsible for the story I created in my head. As I began dating, I realized the perception over time and moved into a new story. By the time I met my husband, I knew instantly I did choose to marry, and I wanted to marry him. I became aware of a new reality. A changed perception allowed me to live out of the story or reality I had created. Little girls become women who either continue the stories, or live out of them into new ones. We choose to lift the brick of artificial perception and move into our interior freedom.

As we age, we live the stories and we live our created realities. We do this consciously and subconsciously. If we believe all of the impossible messages of the media we move into the narratives of meeting impossible measures and standards of "beauty" in terms of weight, breast size, skin tone, hairstyle, and the list goes on. We choose to believe the perceptions as we know the impossible reality of the Barbie image and the size zero message of clothing – very destructive messages, indeed. In fact, some women have created a story of self-perception demanding denial of pleasure from food to obtain these false realities. Many women have learned to associate the sensual pleasure of eating with negative emotions of guilt and shame. Further, women create stories and perceptions which become attitudes toward their bodies as they ruminate about food choices. A woman who enjoys a piece of French Silk Pie must later pay the price as she beats herself up remembering the woes of cellulite. She believes the story of denying pleasure and hating a part of her body.

We stop beating ourselves up. We are gloriously "good enough" – we remove the brick of false perception created by our culture. Women cover their bodies on beaches, afraid they are not beautiful and worried they will never get better. We are already beautiful – in our voluptuous views of self-acceptance. We stop denying our bodies in order to please others, and make decisions only as we need for health and wholeness. Separation is the opposite of connection. Separation is dissonance. Our power and truth come to us in connection and wholeness. My intent is to move us into loving, personal relationship with all parts of self and spirit and into connection with our truth and our grandest stories and possibilities. We choose. We sort our perceptions and examine our being to live out of the stories into new, hope-filled ones. A woman was viciously made fun of in high school, and even ignored – yet she became an excellent brain surgeon. She knew to move out of the stories of her childhood. She changed the perception being shown to others and found others changing the perception they viewed of her as well.

Physical Perceptions

We create stories of our own physical gifts. We notice the multitude of ways a woman's body has beautifully performed during moments of the day when it's *doing*. New stories of love and connection to physical self can be created while doing: riding bike, rollerblading, yoga, making love, and giving birth. ... These are the moments which define the contours of our eloquent physical reality. My body climbed a mountain in Seattle. I could see my breath as I perspired in a t-shirt and enjoyed both the hot and the cool. My body maneuvered a white-water raft in a complete circle atop a rapid, and my body lifted my toddler into the air as I hit the water at the bottom of a waterslide because I promised his face wouldn't go in the water. My body can carry an iced chai latte with one hand, while steering a bicycle with the other. Our bodies are amazing. I learned to waterski when I was forty years old, a time when many women choose to believe the story they are "too old" to continue skiing. In my story, I'm just getting started and have many more experiences ahead of me. Imagine if I believed the stories of my phy-ed teachers through school who told me my body couldn't perform. Our bodies convey freedom. Our bodies proudly carry us through life, if we only let them. We can create the reality and truth of our physical beauty.

Physical health defines our self-concept as we examine the stories or perceptions of what we are able and not able to do. When we feel ill we truly feel separate from our Selves. A fever teaches me to slow down and rest. A stomach discomfort teaches me to watch my diet. While society teaches us to pump up with energy drinks and relax with alcohol, we listen dearly to what our bodies have to say. Our bodies magnificently tell us what we need and if we do not pay attention, they will scream at us in illness. The perceptions of our intellect and emotions rest in our cellular structure – in health or in illness. Our bodies thrive with loving care, and suffer while they teach us important life lessons. We listen to what our bodies need, and change cognition and emotions to resonate with intuitive knowing.

We barely notice our stories unless we fall into difficulty with impairment or illness. I've learned from illness how to view my body as a vessel brilliantly designed for doing, loving and being loved. Sadly, many women accept diagnosis and are affected emotionally with physical limitations. I heard a remarkable speaker, Dr. Carol Ritberger, who is a biomedical intuitive and author of the book *Your Personality Your Health*. I am intrigued with her ability to see people's energy systems and identify physical, emotional, and spiritual causes creating physical destruction, because I intuit the truth of her work. Certainly, genetically, we are predetermined to certain sicknesses; however, it's remarkable to consider the emotional and spiritual components to our physical selves. We are in constant communication with our physical self, thus we need to take care of the messages we send. For example, if I repeatedly tell myself "it is way too much", or that "life is a struggle", my body repeatedly is receiving a stressful, negative message. Over time, we hold our stress in our predisposed personality or area and eventually our bodies cry out in one form or another for healing.

We are in a constant dynamic of destroying or healing our physical selves, regardless of age or circumstance. I see women giving up and omitting life experiences due to aging and I want to shake them out of their despondency and show them another story leading to strength and power. Later chapters in this book examine healing as pertains to our personal relationship and journey with our physical, mental/emotional and spiritual existence. Treating our bodies well diminishes the cellular destruction caused by stress and allows us to know our beauty, and identify each body part in a loving manner in terms of what it is able to do and feel.

Intellectual Perceptions

Our intellectual self is, in fact, genetically created. IQ is inborn and we are either underachievers or overachievers. The stories and perceptions we create in regard to our intelligence can create self-fulfilling prophecies of destruction or limitless growth. I'm a horrible test-taker ... what if I believed the limitations of tests? Clearly, we need to create narratives where we are not so hard on ourselves and where we recognize intellectual gift. Diverse learning styles exist and we cannot fall into measurements and tests of what we don't know as perceptions of self--another brick in the wall of limitation. Rather, we measure what we *do* know, realizing we have a whole lifetime to choose what else we find significant to put into intellect. I applaud the work of Howard Gardner, a Harvard educator who devised a theory of nine multiple intelligences or learning styles. Students deserve to know their way of being brilliant – especially as society labels and medicates those who don't learn in a manner of sitting in complacency to lowest level of intellect – knowledge spewed forth with no promise of integration. Mike didn't succeed with traditional measures of academic success, but he became the lead in a play I directed. I watched as audience members pointed and whispered in disbelief and amazement, viewing his true intellect and magnificence. Mike moved into an experience of his brilliance from being on stage. We look for opportunities to define our brilliance and create perceptions of truth and success of our individual giftedness. Definitions of intellect present themselves in our experiential knowing, and are not confined to textbooks, tests, or even degrees. We are lifelong learners capable of embracing profound wisdom of knowing how we magnificently shine only by exposing ourselves to opportunities of knowing excellence. … As women, it's likely that we've developed our stories of failure from people who didn't recognize our manner of learning. I admire non-traditional women who return to college because they know how to create stories and perceptions of success. They return to college because they know who they are *not*, and are growing into who they *are*. Intellect is defined throughout life as we are shaped into our giftedness. We define our intellect by our *wisdom* of experiential knowing.

My kindergarten teacher gave me horrid remarks on my grade report because I couldn't sit still. What if I believed I were horrid? My first grade teacher told me I was a cheater, what if I believed I were dishonest? My first grade teacher, second grade Sunday school teacher, and eighth grade phy-ed teacher (yeah, the list goes on) constantly punished me for talking and giggling. What if I believed I needed to quiet my voice and stop my laughter? I see women destroyed by the unhealthy comments of others, especially unprofessional educators, who told them they couldn't. I sat through a speech given through tears so a woman would remember her worth after she received a thorough verbal beating from an instructor who said she was a failure at public speaking. How dare women evaluate themselves based only on a few negative perceptions when they've truly given effort!

And I still refuse to sit still when women suffer false realities and narratives of others' perceptions. It's time to create new ones of inner wisdom. We choose to live out of the stories of judgment. Everyone is gifted and life brings opportunity to discovery profound knowing. Each time we learn we are changing our perceptions. *Wisdom* is how we measure intellectual success.

Intellectual Perceptions or Emotional Perceptions?

"You smouth!", shouted the librarian. The group of children giggled, knowing she'd intended to say, "smart mouth", but her bright, red lipstick and pointed finger were way too caught up with the issue of the overdue books. Her overall manner was likened to the authority figures of internment camps, and students avoided spending time in the library during her shift. Getting along well with others through communication excellence affects our ability to meet goals for success – and happiness in vocation. Those who stomp feet in anger, yell at coworkers with demeaning tone, or isolate themselves in pain are not perceived as "teamplayers." More importantly, they are also never the ones we turn to, trust, count on, or look up to as mentors. In fact, negative emotional energy in the workplace and in our personal lives is always destructive – unless we use our inner wisdom to allow transformation and growth.

Negative energy reminds me of Chris – because I allowed her to get to my emotional health. It was my junior year of college and three roommates and I frequently enjoyed the friendship of the landlords and their young children in the floor below. When Chris moved in, everything changed. Our laughter was replaced with tension. She stomped, she screamed, she emitted anger while clenching teeth. Lights shook below while stomps reverberated in young children's bedrooms. Finally, we held a meeting and pleaded a warning. The following morning she had a tantrum because she couldn't find her hairbrush – her flannel pajamas with pink flowers contrasted with her red-faced screaming. That did it. The same evening we threw a huge party and invited everyone we knew. When she arrived, she asked why we were having the party, and we told her. It was an eviction party. Hers.

Sometimes we need to evict others from our mental space, especially those who know how to push our buttons. Failure to evict them from our focus can send us into reactions or irrational behavior. We cannot control the other, but we can absolutely control choice of reaction. We recognize causes of consequence and regret, and listen to messages our body sends us to arise with power intact. Life experience presents intense moments when we are absolutely out of control and we are grasping for something, anything, anyone to control in our misconstrued view. Moments of white flash anger, freaked out nerves, and rapid, uneven breathing send us places we do not emotionally want to go. We maintain our dignity. Society views people who are unable to control their emotions as irrational or immature – and undignified. I once walked in on someone just as his face turned red, a vein on his forehead began to throb, and he threw valuable blueprints while he shouted. Dignity and grace are achieved only when we awaken to sensory signals challenging our restraint.

"Emotional hijacking" (Goleman) occurs because our bodies are literally sending more blood to the emotional or frontal (limbic) parts of our brain than to the left brain of our rational thought. Goleman states:

> ***Take the power of emotions to disrupt thinking itself. Neuroscientists use the term "working memory" for the capacity of attention that holds in mind the facts essential for completing a given task or problem. … But circuits from the limbic brain to the prefrontal lobes mean that the signals of strong emotion – anxiety, anger, and the***

> ***like – can create neural static, sabotaging the ability of the prefrontal lobe to maintain working memory. That is why when we are emotionally upset we say we "just can't think straight" – and why continual emotional distress can create deficits in a child's intellectual abilities, crippling the capacity to learn.*** – Dan Goleman, *Emotional Intelligence*

As a child, I had a pattern of screaming, running down the hall to my room, slamming my door, and throwing myself on my bed to cry. This behavior served me well as a child, but tears of anger at work made me unable to speak and I felt my voice slipping away. We are at an emotional crossroads. We can choose growing edges of calming and coping or decisions based on overriding emotions sabotaging our ability to move into true power and limitless potential.

Moments of conflict with others bring us to emotional override because our souls are screaming in pain. How many of us dare stop and listen in order to name the pain? Conflict with others is always calling us to notice unresolved, unspoken pain of relationship with self. If we can calm, we can name what our souls need: dignity, love, trust, or worth. We can frame our words to heal the pain and gain what we need, but only if we move into the opportunity of solitude and knowing face-to-face moments with our souls. Our worth is formed in our calm abiding and resolutions toward healing, not our attempts to overpower or win or submit: bandages of temporary conflict resolution rather than true wholeness and empowerment.

Angry words and actions result in broken relationships, regret, and even legal consequences when anger becomes violence. Anger is an emotion that serves us only briefly as we sense the injustice, unfairness, point of conflict. Remaining in anger always creates harm for our bodies (and relationships). We learn balance. We cool down going for a walk, or weightlifting, or writing letters to be ripped up in order to name our needs. We work through the emotion and return to rational thought. This is our coping. Emotions are never wrong to feel, but remaining in them longer than necessary is useless to our being and, ultimately, creates paralysis rather than growth.

Char's disappointment was fed by the belief that even her own son judged her and didn't see her value. She spoke, "Nobody is giving me a break! I work and I work and I am overwhelmed because nobody in my family or my job is giving me any slack! I am so afraid I'm turning into a bitch, yet I can't stop it until somebody, anybody, gives me a break!" Her words struck a chord, because I remember feeling similarly. Indeed, nobody *is* going to give us a break--so we live empowered and **take the break**. We take the break, and restore our power. Char *knew* this in the moment when reality and soul connected in tears. If we don't listen to our souls, they often show themselves and scream to be noticed as tears stream down our faces.

Tears are necessary to our being and our healing. Our culture still sends stories relating tears to perceptions of weakness. We stifle young boys when they cry teaching suppression of tears and avoidance of emotional pain. They learn to "buck up", but at what expense? Girls cry, yet women who do fight perceptions of being "hormonal" or "overly sensitive" which is somehow equated with a lack of power. Moments of tears are, in fact, cathartic. They cleanse our bodies of toxins and stress and we just plain feel good when we are finished, while lying on wet pillows licking the salt from our cheeks. Tears are healing. My current work with spiritual direction and conflict resolution often brings tears in the exact moment of pain. It is in the crisis or opportunity of this moment the other names the pain and moves into associating needs for healing. Our tears teach us instantly and exponentially what we need. We listen to tears to rise up out of the sadness and into health. Tears are opportunity to transform. The culmination of our intellectual, physical, and emotional narrative creates our state of being. Being connected with our state of being brings us the familiarity of *remembering* our truth. We are at home.

We break the cycle of negativity to maintain our true state of being. Living in this world exposes us to a barrage of experiences and perceptions. As we proceed through life's journey, we often endure sufferings and tragedies that may or may not balance or harmonize with life's joy. We need to take such care of our being. We can be drawn into the horrific stories of the media that teaches us to always be very, very afraid of our weather, our war, and terrorists. We can easily fall into a global depression as we view the social injustices of our world. We maintain the dignity of our true state with authentic perceptions replacing the "reality" presented in our media. News perceptions are politically and strategically marketed toward someone else's reality and political gain and need not compromise our emotional well-being and hope. We dare choose realities of a truth deeper than the ignorance of a culture and its media.

We choose to move into a more compassionate and loving experience when we spend time with our selves and our emotional stresses, which would otherwise keep us from our state of being and our calm. Our calm urges us to learn and grow rather than to hide from the pain of our experience; we learn to use silence to dare face our hurt and move through the pain into the transformation of our grief. The Chinese character for crisis also contains the character of opportunity. In our moments of deepest suffering we are transformed into so much more than we ever knew we could be, if we allow the opportunity of growth. Truly, people who've hurt us or left us can indeed be the very lesson to our next path to happiness and power. We protect our hearts and our power.

Life changes our perceptions. When we understand our Selves, we know what we need in our relationships and we present ourselves to others, engaging in the joy we have to offer. We embrace the power of connection with loving relationships, as is the case with significant others and dearest friends. When I was twelve, I met my best friend, Lisa. I admired her ability to be a social leader, and we seemed to truly understand each other at an emotional level. Our many sleepovers often consisted of us discussing our current crushes and our endless frustration of waiting for boys to fall desperately in love with us.

We would talk until we were ready to scream into pillows. Then we would scream all of our young angst into pillows until we began laughing. These sessions always ended up in uncontrollable laughter. Our malts and pizza evolved into the college experiences of beer and pizza and we continued to be inseparable. We continued to scream and laugh together and love life even as we moved into our adult life experiences with husbands, families, and houses. I know I am blessed to have known her. I look for my own children to find one person who believes in them and understands their emotions while laughing with them and letting them be who they are. We should all be so lucky to scream into pillows to let go of our problems until we can laugh with relief and the calm of knowing it's all okay and we aren't alone after all.

Mindful Perceptions and Beholding

Chaos of society's demands moves us into moments when we need someone, anyone to cut us some slack. We fully awaken to the realization that only we can fill ourselves by sorting through the chaos. We catch the inaccuracies of negative perceptions we created from our looking glass selves and we let go. We do this only when we move out of the chaos and busyness of our culture and into the mindful clarity of self-love. We unclutter the chaos and discover interior freedom and joy.

Choosing the path to affect life and live passionately lies in our ability to observe our deepest ability to love self within our hearts and souls, an awakening of passion. A mindful lens allows us to hold the little girl who didn't deserve negative perception and message so destruction stops and healing begins. We hug the little girl we were and we kiss her, and we reassure her we will never again listen to those perceptions. We assure her of her worth with each kiss of clarity and promise to heal the perceptions. She smiles because she sees us letting go of artificial perceptions that no longer serve us and replacing them with mantras of self-love and acceptance. We remove the brick and trust the new vision opening before us.

Beholders understand there are no limitations – limitations are perceived and have no power. We protect our power and refuse unhealthy removal of our power. Indeed, we move into the transcendent knowing of our emotional needs which identifies healthy and unhealthy words and behaviors. We struggle with the transcendent sufferings and move into a deeper knowledge of our emotional needs. Anais Nin, my favorite writer, writes with such passion and emotional immediacy, a style she verbalized as a spiritual place of *beyond rational*. We are literally moving out of the rational thought that drives most of our existence and into a *beyond rational* place where our feelings and intuition have power and we exemplify highly creative beauty. We are beautifully created and we create beautifully.

The Baz Luhrman quotation at the beginning of the chapter urges us to do something which scares us everyday. We face our fears and evoke our power. We are risk-takers who dare do the face-to-face with intuitive self. Our inner child and soul calls us into removing our fears and returning to our play. We move beyond our emotions into the intuitive place that guides us to our greatness, our happiness, and our unfathomable potential to be loved and to love. Dare to live life passionately.

> ***The more accelerated our life becomes, the more we have to learn to select only the essential, to create our own repose and meditation islands within an uncluttered mental space.*** – Anais Nin, *The Novel of the Future*

Chapter Two

Kissing Ourselves All Over

I realized a long time ago that a belief which does not spring from conviction in the emotions is no belief at all.
– Evelyn Scott

Woman is more filled than man to make exploration and take bolder action in nonviolence ... there is no occasion for women to consider themselves subordinate or inferior to man. ... Woman is the companion of man, gifted with equal mental capacity. ... If by strength is meant moral power, then woman is immeasurably man's superior. ... If nonviolence is the law of our being, the future is with women. – Ghandi

The nude statue in the exhibit was of a man and a woman touching in the moment just before a kiss. The clarity of genius design created an artwork perceived as ice or glass, though it could not melt or break – scientifically remarkable. *Beyond science.* The chasms and carvings reflected luminous radiance and aesthetically altering hues. Intellectual appreciation blended with inner awakenings and stirrings in my heart as I viewed such exquisite form of romantic love. First kisses danced in my heart and head. Suddenly three-dimensional intrigue gained even deeper knowing as the pedestal began to revolve and connect with sunlight dancing through texture and created clarity. His and her expression of wonderment toward the other awakened a spiritual moment of beauty with awesome remembrance of head and heart receiving: a moment of perfection. I paid attention because it spoke to my deepest value: unconditional love. Loving ourselves unconditionally teaches us to notice those who remember the exquisite gentleness of compassionate, loving perspective. We learn to see loving experiences lined up and created specifically, as personal gifts of affirmation. We savor the experience of falling in love with ourselves. Indeed, we become art no longer able to stand still in our beauty. We begin to dance and move amidst luminous colors of sunlight moving through individual chasms and created design of interior countenance. Our lives become meaningfully connected and we become the interconnections of countenance we brilliantly were meant to shine. We value our selves differently as woman in love.

Knowing: Validation vs. Affirmation

We value being liked and being validated by others. Jason was a student mainstreamed into my classroom at a high school many years ago. His "speech" was to read five sentences to the class. He was a Special Needs student and this was his level of learning. His face intensely studied the words on the white notecards and his every facial muscle showed the tension and focus toward needing to succeed. Immediately upon finishing, he stiffly held his body and the notecards just as they were – but he sharply lifted his head and looked to the audience ... searching for a response to his vulnerable situation. It touches my heart to remember the thunderous applause he received. His face broke into a brilliant smile – complete happiness. They validated his worth.

We face our world in much the same manner public speaking students face an audience – we are either "on" or "off" according to response. Self-love allows us to be "on". We learn excellence in charisma and nonverbal/verbal congruity while we speak – while we rely on audience feedback to determine the impact of our message. We live a life of paying attention. We sort our intent to live as catalysts who send intent and good to others. Focusing on personal relationship and inner being creates a love that mindfully carries us into knowing goodness. When we allow the mirror of our thought to reflect narratives of love and positivity we no longer *need validation*, rather we *celebrate affirmation*.

Mignon McLaughlin once said "A successful marriage requires falling in love many times, always with the same person." We commit to falling in love many times, with the same person … our intuited beings of truth. A personal relationship of commitment calls us to recognize affirmations as the intimate steps of our journey of interconnectedness and value.

Value Formation and Wholeness

Taking time to know ourselves intimately establishes the precious relationship opportunity for unconditional love and acceptance. We sense our attitudes and form our value systems from them. For example, I suffer side effects from certain preservatives. This sensitivity creates an attitude of dislike for foods and medications containing the potential uncomfortable side effects. Thus, I value natural foods and healing and use medications only as necessary to my well-being. Time and experiences of stomach discomfort and wanting to clear the spider webs of unclear thought were adverse experiences birthing and forming layers to shape the value of organic diet and healing. It's taken literally about twenty years to bring me to this place, and the value is preciously mine – I own it. Just as you own attitudes/dislikes and value systems from the history of your experience. We hold them dear because our cognition has repetitive thought working toward living the experience or story in a unique manner.

Two individuals cannot have the exact value system because of experiential differences. Lawrence Kohlberg, a professor from Harvard, identifies a framework of stages for value formation. It's imperative we know our value systems to understand our self-perceptions and return to wholeness more clearly. He states we view our reality or truth from the following perspectives: pre-conventional morality, conventional morality and postconventional morality.

For any given topic we have a value system response from the aforementioned perspectives. Because of our complex belief systems, we literally engage ourselves in a variety of perspectives for any given topic. In other words, we remain in preconventional morality for some aspects of our lives, while growing into latter stages for other aspects of our experience. We learn **preconventional morality** as children. Preconventional morality is doing "good" simply to receive reward rather than punishment. Children in gradeschool classrooms collect one hundred M&M's for being good one hundred days simply to be rewarded with a party when one hundred M&M's have been gathered, while losing tickets as consequence for "bad behavior" or mistakes of talking out of turn or treating others unfairly. Adults remain in preconventional morality for some aspects of their lives. Parking tickets are an example of punishment. I run to my car with arms full of boxes, bags and purse just to avoid the $25 fine I'll receive if the quarter for my limited parking minutes expires on days I need to use metered parking.

Conventional Morality drives much of our decision-making and value perspectives. Following rules or regulations of structures or establishments (systems) can give us great ease and comfort, rather than chaos and confusion. We obey the speed limit to avoid speeding tickets and accidents. We work with the ethics and expectations specified in our job descriptions and mission statements. We parent according to the expectations of the morals created in our specific society and culture. We pay our bills, fulfill our obligations and civic responsibilities in the manner to which we've been told. We support our troops because they are acting within the expectations of our governmental system. People remain in conventional belief when they choose to join others (who view in similar manner) for group affiliations and religious establishments. We rise to the standards of a civic society and do our part to maintain the integrity of successful systems or conventions. However; in meaningful aspects to our lives, we may seek more depth of living out value. Personal relationship with spirit is one such place … indeed, the root of our existence.

Postconventional Morality is a perspective of moving into individual ownership of a value that may not be commonly accepted, while seeking "greater good" than conventional law or policy dictates. The comfort zone provided by our systems is the greatest barrier to our movement to this level. However, meaningful issues of value deserve a critical approach of movement away from establishment in order to question and sort and discover authenticity. We return with an ownership of values from experiential knowing and wisdom. Indeed, in cases of religious establishment, those moving through motions are missing out on deeper engagement or embracing of the community of values. It's the difference between *knowing* and *knowing about.* I am old enough to have moved from listening to my favorite music on vinyl albums into the age of c-d's. I tell my students the difference between the sound of a c-d vs. the sound of an album. A c-d lacks the rich, full sound of an album, but their experience only involves knowing c-d's and knowing about albums from the stories of my generation. The warmth of a stylus on a turntable gently dropping to engage vinyl in a production of fullness of sound can only be gained through experiential *knowing.* They perhaps believe my value as truth, but if they experienced the difference in quality, they would embrace the value more fully in their *knowing.*

Religious establishments are intriguing examples. Many go through the motions of the convention, but movement away to examine, sort, experience and own the values of the religion arrives at a full embracing and living of the religion: a difference between *knowing about* a God and *knowing* God experientially. Religions thrive when they are authentically experienced by each member. We critically sort meaningful values in order to own them, and embrace them in meaningful manner – rather than simply going through the motions or knowing about. We experience goodness. As Merton states:

> ***I do not intend to divorce myself at any point from Catholic tradition. But neither do I intend to accept points of that tradition blindly, and without understanding, and without making them really my own. For it seems to me that the first responsibility of a man of faith is to make his faith really part of his own life, not by rationalizing it but by living it.*** – Thomas Merton, *No Man is an Island*

Unconditional love toward establishments we *know* gives us perspective to discern acceptance and change within the value structure. Our perspective guides us to a humanitarian level of changing policy or establishment, a Higher Good should prevail as extensions of our newly discovered goodness and views formed in unconditional love. The controversy of our present nation at war well-represents the many who've moved into a desire for peace as perspective rather than remain with the decisions of our political system which, in the eyes of an increasing many, is bringing needless killing of innocent victims. Social movements of the sixties against the Vietnam War brought us a plethora of musical messages, *Life* magazine photos, and university policy against protestors representing the varying perspectives of the culture. The contemporary song "American Idiot" by Greenday mirrors the same sentiment – questioning present policy and media messages of fear – meant to motivate us to "fight for peace". We examine our views:

Don't want to be an Amercan idiot.
One nation controlled by the media.
Information age of hysteria.
It's going out to idiot America (American Idiot, 2004).

We are not idiots, we are critical thinkers who examine beliefs and return to perspectives invigorated by the passion of our deepest wholeness: our actions become extensions of our beliefs. We are not paralyzed or helpless. We are not stuck. We trust voices of dissonance and listen to intuitive self. Our gut reminds us to act in love and compassion. We support troops because we love those who protect us as we strive for a Higher Good of peace derived from understanding, connectedness and resolution with others. A GI Joe doll sits in a dorm waiting for its owner's return from Iraq. A best friend's toy is transformed into a physical presence of loving remembrance and hope.

We listen to ourselves differently when we notice our soul in order to critically sort and find our Higher Good of being. We return to ourselves, more richly, warmly embracing. We grow in intimate relationship and unconditional love – deepest value formation. We resolve conflict of self vs. inner self each time we set boundaries of values or critically sort to know transcendent values of Higher Good, so our actions are extensions of our goodness. Harmony rather than dissonance. Healing rather than conflict.

Taking our values to others presents a new view of conflict: differing values and perceptions bring us to confusion rather than clarity. Again, we listen to inner voices to resolve external conflict. We dare face the dissonance to achieve harmony. I once traveled to New York City with a dear friend. Windy conditions forced us to take a standby flight and we arrived extremely late to make the 8:00 show we'd reserved tickets to see. The city bus we boarded needed to make stops and would never allow us to meet our deadline. So I got off the bus, at night, my first time in New York City.

My friend hesitantly followed my decision. The safety of the bus was clearly the rational choice (her choice) after a chaotic day of travel. To make the situation worse, long lines of people were hailing cabs … cabs were no longer an option. So we walked one mile, at night, in New York City with luggage and heightened senses. We reached the theatre at exactly 8:00, and I still remember the thrill of conquering odds and arriving – but my friend didn't share my excitement.

Our differing values presented themselves again the following day at the Statue of Liberty. Back then, tourists could climb to the top of her copper crown and view the city. By the time we arrived, the staircase closed to ensure everyone met the last ferry thirty minutes later – a rule. It was my birthday and I was a runner so I knew I could run-up, view the city, and run back down. I questioned the rule and my friend had had enough. She burst out, "You're a rule-breaker, aren't you?"

I gasped and looked at her. "You follow rules, don't you?"

Guess what? We incorporate both perspectives as we sort our true power. We need both personalities of people. Rebels are catalysts for change and organizers create the change. Rule-followers are necessary to prevent chaos. Rules retain the sanctity of my marriage and protect me as I achieve goals of my career. Discernment teaches us to know when to rebel and when to follow rules. A guy chained to a tree to protest an issue may be acting from profound core belief or merely gaining the attention of the media. Blindly following rules and others is as ridiculous as the shallow plea for attention. When we empower ourselves to critically sort our beliefs and involve heartfelt discernment of information, we rise to authentic beliefs and actions. We know *why* we believe what we believe with controversial issues. Further, we *embrace* the rules of systems in community with others by *owning* beliefs of workplace systems, governmental policies, and religious establishments. Actions are extensions of our focused passion, and we love ourselves for *living out* beliefs and speaking *true voice*.

We all are familiar with imposters who pretend to live out values, but are unstable and inconsistent. Empathy is formed when we are toddlers, and some people are victims – and do not own the emotional equipment necessary to form deep emotional belief systems. Likely, the energy of these people will continue to be destructive and dissonant. We rise to the fortune and gift of our authenticity. Women who know compassion and unconditional love as they shape belief systems needn't concern themselves with those who cannot change. We become attracted to others and surround ourselves intuiting who is about good. We learn from our error--knowing we are imperfect as we become excellent. The rules we live by are the boundaries we learn throughout life to protect our wholeness. Becoming true is our nature and we can love ourselves fully and unconditionally: our bodies become sacred instruments magnificently performing random and intentional acts of kindness and ethics; and our voice is rooted in Truth. We bring synergy to others.

Barriers to Valuing Personal Relationship with Self

It's easy to see distinctly when issues arise between right and wrong (and **choosing** the right path is still not always easy). We become wiser as we discern our value structure. Developing trust gives rational perception to risk, rather than paralysis of fear. We dare move out of our comfort zones. Discernment teaches individual power, movement, and commitment to self. We become entrepeneurs who take risks because we learn to trust our decisions. Wholeness is power.

Change seems frightening. Our comfort zone is created by the behaviors and decisions manifested from our thoughts and beliefs. Even if we are not currently satisfied, we may enjoy the comfort of knowing familiarity and routine. Unsatisfied people walk around with tunnel vision of dischord, as if they have no power to change. Change **is** risky. It can cost us, but we are worth it. Every time. There is no growth without change.

Individual power is birthed when we stop deceiving ourselves and begin believing our Selves. The word *ethics* is derived from Aristotle's *ethos*, which means credibility or believability. In Aristotle's time, good character could quite literally save one's life. In our current time, good character is imperative to lifelong healing. Further, good character saves one's integrity, value, and Self (in the context of wholistic health: mental/emotional, intellectual, physical, and spiritual). We are busy being pushed to make decisions, being stuck in places we do not want to be, and being worried or afraid of doing anything different. So we compromise our integrity because the cost of losing this value seems so much more convenient, so much easier than living our integrity. Unfortunately, we end up costing our very Selves over time. We lose the ability to be able to be alone with ourselves, we lose the ability to sleep at night because of the decisions we've made, and we lose the ability to grandly love ourselves with ultimate acceptance of human failing as we strive toward our deepest integrity.

Women walk a tightrope balancing cost of personal power with cost of time to commit to the work of personal relationship and falling in love with self. Awareness in hearts shouts an imbalance of truth not yet realized – a major cost that will not diminish if not paid attention to. Merton, a Trappist monk, wrote of learning to "pronounce ourselves" with true voice. We take the time, though our society seems to prevent our very doing so. We live in a technological chaos of e-mails, cellphones, word processing, and meetings. Our busyness prevents us from thinking, from knowing different values, from considering other viewpoints.

I once enrolled in a health program with expectations of exercising on a daily basis to improve heart health and body composition. I exercised anyway, so the time cost was not a concern. When I discovered I had to wear a pedometer daily for a year, and record how many steps I'd taken daily … aaugghhh … record-keeping! I quit. I wanted to pursue the healthy cause, but simply saw the details as too time-consuming, and I was deceiving myself to think I could comply with the expectations. We empty ourselves on a daily basis, as we listen in silence to our intuitive self. We let go of what we can to prevent draining ourselves with responsibilities and overwhelming fears there will not be enough time. We fill ourselves with clarity of how we use our time. We view time in a different manner and commit to our growth. We choose perspective to view time from a spiritual sense, an immeasurable value to our energy systems. We are currently depleted rather than filled because we are not getting to our Selves. We fill with energy each and every moment we are listening in our hearts. Time from this perspective provides a multitude of possibility and power – at the expense of only a few minutes of earthly-measured time. We define time by our self-love.

A second barrier to unconditional love of self is our complacency. It's easier not to … always. It simply takes work to grow. I know I shouldn't eat fatty foods, but the availability still attracts me, and I recently put off a cholesterol test because I didn't want to give up the butter and rich sauces I enjoy. Coffee and energy drinks are causing society to become agitated rather than relaxed, but it's much easier to grab a quick, short-term fix to avoid suffering headaches and fatigue of withdrawal rather than spending time learning to relax and sleep well. It's easier to not talk about sex than to face the very real dangers facing college women today.

We commit to our worth because of our inner knowing. Ethical and loving thought patterns create our being and our doing. We choose to create our reality and stay there unless seduced into change. Works of art: movies, books, and artistic creations can serve to move us. When we are touched in our hearts, we move into our heads and justify whether we can accept another's truth. Karlyn Kohrs-Campbell, University of Minnesota, refers to this as "virtual experience". Dr. Campbell researches rhetorical criticism and theory, political communication, women's communication and social movement. Her expertise guides understanding of how women shape the "virtual experience" of their truth within our social structures. Rhetors (persuaders) "call up ideas, pictures, and experiences in those they address" (9). A virtual *reality* in the sensual images presented becomes choice for us to accept or reject as we create our own definition of reality. We are taken into a potential vehicle of persuasion and if we *see* their truth, and *accept* their truth we *change*. The truth of our inner power paints a virtual reality more emotionally and logically convincing than our present truth – and falling in love with ourselves outweighs any challenges or barriers to change. *We must construct a narrative of the same reality – we create realities of empowerment and self-love.* We channel our energy into moving toward good rather than dissipation or depletion. The journey of this book is to face the values and perspectives in stories about our Selves and others and to dare to take the time to remove barriers of views that don't serve our growth, creating a new vision of authentic character, integrity, and self-love.

Valuing Self into Personal Loving Relationship

We break up or end friendships with others who do not reciprocate kindness and love (or, at least, we *should*). Interestingly, we do not treat our personal relationship with Self in the same manner. A perspective of a dualistic relationship of woman and her spirit calls us to examine how we treat ourselves. How do we speak to ourselves? Do we neglect or even intentionally avoid spending time or desiring more with our Self? Our desire to be "okay", our desire to please others may, in fact, keep us from growing into love and from being able to like our aloneness. It's ironic that we settle for less within our own company of self than we would ever accept from another. Our personal relationship with self deserves and demands attention. We dare face the brokenness in order to move into wholeness.

Compromised Integrity

On the computer desk in my office there is a yellow post-it note that says simply: "Compromised Integrity". Dr. Carol Ritberger, a biomedical intuitive, spoke these words to me as she discussed the various aspects of my healing. I've thought, meditated, and prayed on these words for quite some time. They represent every woman's need for personal power and truth. She spoke just what I needed to hear and I committed to the work of responding and discerning … magnificently aware of my own healing.

Numbness derived from chaos and disorder creates paralysis. Silence builds interior boundaries from clarity. When we become complacent or "stuck" in life we make no decisions. However; by making no decisions we are, indeed, still making a decision. We are deciding to let life happen to us, rather than moving into a place where we can happen to life and live our passion. Each time we allow ourselves to divide our passion and energy, we lose our power. The word *worry* is derived from a root word meaning "divided energy". Worry is taking half of our power. Our fear distracts us from our focus, and, again, we lose our power. When we spend no time with our Selves, we cannot build the loving personal relationship we deserve, which is our greatest power. We are at a crossroads.

Additionally, we become too busy to notice when others are taking our power. We can allow others to make us feel less, or to feel we do not have value. We are ruining our beautiful narratives. Our reality needs to include time with our aloneness to know our Selves deeply and honestly. Then we know to recognize others or situations which wish to take our power and we choose. We choose to keep it. We move to the grandest vision of our reality, which is our loving relationships, with self full of acceptance and admiration. Because we recongize areas of unhealing, areas of negative self-talk from guilt, shame, and fear, we can sort through and move into positivity and transformation. Self-acceptance replaces beating ourselves up and we find ourselves falling in love with the spirit within. Women in love cannot help but be inspired to perform random and intentional acts of compassion. *Knowing* experiences of grandest self-love leads us to regard body as sacred instrument to perform loving actions of kindness. We grow in vision of our loveliness and take our countenance of love and compassion out to others. We move from complacency to decision-making and in order to affect earthly existence. We affect the world with our power.

We've become too rational. We spend time justifying our actions and decisions to our self and to others at the expense of listening to our truest needs. What we need to do is move into a deeper recognition of our spirit. We move from our heads (rational self) to our hearts where our emotions and intuition guide, and back to our heads with new vision that is "beyond rational". We need to let go of proving. We've nothing to prove when we know our integrity and character. We know our love.

In our heads we justify. My husband and I just bought a convertible. Some of our friends were surprised at the decision, and I found myself justifying the price, the gas mileage, and any other reasons that could inductively move everyone to see that a convertible was a good decision. The truth is that my son who loves cars saw it and loved it. He then showed it to me, and I immediately loved it – it represented fun at a time when we needed fun, it was colored with champagne and tortoise (faux), which was visually appealing to me, and I wanted to see my husband driving around and enjoying the world in it. I laugh now when I realize I gave only the rational reasons, as if it matters what others think of our car choice. *As if it matters what others think.* We so easily fall into justifying. Our true guide for personal journey can only be felt.

In our hearts, we experience our emotions. Our emotions teach us and guide us. They show us what we need to face bravely, what we need from others, what we need from our Selves. When we neglect our emotional needs, we neglect our very being. We cannot move forward toward any goals, because we do not even know our wants. In our silence, we move into our hearts. We think, we meditate. We find. The following chapter speaks of the magnificence we find as we also encounter our spirit and Higher Good when we move into our hearts. Our hearts guide us to our intuition. Our gut knows when life is right, or when life is misguided. Our intuitive self guides us primitively and strongly away from danger and unhealthy people, unhealthy decisions, and into our deepest integrity – our power of being who we are meant to be.

The truest being of our Self is our value. We lovingly look to guide the beauty of our being toward deeper truth, toward deeper love, toward deeper acceptance. We find we've changed. We find we've moved. When we move back into our head we see ourselves differently. We realize we are better than okay. We realize we are enough without being perfect. We excellently are. We no longer look to others for validation because we are affirmed in relation to Self and/or Higher Good. Others simply and delightfully affirm that which we already know: our authentic character, our integrity, and our love.

The poignant words of Marianne Williamson from *A Return to Love* (1992) remind us to stop deceiving ourselves and to live our truth:

We ask ourselves, "Who am I to be brilliant,
Gorgeous,
Talented and fabulous?"
Actually, who are you not to be?
You are a child of God.
Your playing small doesn't serve the world.

Let go of your fear. Grow into love.

Chapter Three:

Silent Messages and Souls Touching

God gave man two ears and one tongue so that we listen twice as much as we speak. – Mark Twain

Listening is a magnetic and strange thing, a creative force. The friends who listen to us are the ones we move toward. When we are listened to, it creates us, makes us unfold and expand. – Anonymous

It's summer and I am sitting on a wicker chair on my porch with a cup of creamy hot cocoa and a peanut butter cookie. A storm is brewing and I'm watching dark clouds roll in and feeling the temperature drop. I smell the rain crossing the field in a sheet of power. Lightning flickers so quickly I cannot see the bolt – it momentarily surrounds me with its static energy. I hear the crack of thunder that shakes the very world around me. I love the sensuality of this moment. Every sense is provided with such stimulation as the rhythm of nature takes full force. I am alive when I am sensually aware. Our senses so accurately serve us with connection to our world.

My perception of listening is a bit unique. My mother went blind when I was nine. I learned to appreciate a connection through shared aural experience, whether it was her classical piano music, my favorite Eric Carmen album, or a performance of Handel's *The Messiah.* In turn, I learned to be her vision and to be aware of the beauty in nature. I tried to capture for her the eloquent lavender and peach beauty of an Austrian iris, or the blue of the green grass in Kentucky, or the azure sky moving into the crimson of a sunset. The verdant images and fragrances of nature nudged me and I listened and noticed to create images and loveliness for her.

My mother was an admirable woman who "saw" with her other senses and was able to be quite independent. Miraculously, she developed the skill to play piano by listening, though she'd been taught to play by sight. She died twenty-five years ago, but I still play her piano in my own home with the music still connecting us. I don't need to see her to be with her. I need only to listen and notice and recognize her remaining essence.

She listened and found hope and goodness. I believe in listening as she did, without judgement, as children and students in my world paint canvases of ideas with their unique words, ideas and passions. I listen and guide their power of independent thought and vision. One student is healing from her service in Iraq. Another student dreams of flying an airplane after a degree in aviation – and she wants to change history, like Amelia Earhart. Another student is embracing college experience after a tragic car accident and long duration of therapy – celebrating arrival to this next place in life. I listen to the colors and strokes they paint in their experience. Truly, a blind person taught me to listen to others and to "see" through the lens of each reality. We can open ourselves up to the beauty of the moment and the other by paying attention and listening.

We all can aspire to sense the beauty of listening to ourselves, to others, and to our world. We spend 80-90% of each day listening to media, family, co-workers, and friends. We can enhance the quality of our lives by paying attention and learning to interpret. Listening is infinitely more than hearing. Hearing is *involuntary*. When a cellphone rings we involuntarily hear it's unique ring. Technically hearing is:

> ***The vibrations move from the middle ear through the snail-shaped, fluid-filled inner ear called the cochlea. The microscopic hair cells in the cochlea convert the fluid movement into electrical energy. This energy is transmitted by the hair cells to the hearing or auditory nerve. The auditory nerve automatically sends electrical signals to our brains*** – Educational Handout, *Awaken Your Sense of Listening*

It's basic science of human anatomy. Unless we have a physical limitation, we will hear a sound, thus it requires no energy or work. Hearing just *is*. We become so much more when we engage ourselves in listening.

Listening is a *choice*. Listening involves recognition, comprehension, interpretation and analysis, and appropriate response. Whew. Listening requires a great deal of energy and work; however we seldom learn to improve the most important communicative aspect of our day. Clearly, when we pay attention to the 80-90% of our day that we listen, we improve the quality of life. We continue to clear the dissonance of our self-talk in order to be fully present to others. We give and we receive when we listen well. We pay attention to others each time, because that is gift. The divorce rate is still at an astounding rate. It's remarkable how many spouses and significant others don't feel listened to … ironically, they are not being paid attention to, resulting in feelings of insignificance. Listening workshops brought into Fortune 500 companies save dollars wasted from poor listening and ensure coworkers are getting along, thus creating less employee turnover. We are all taught to read, to write, to speak – but seldom taught to listen! Yet we are expected to do so each time we engage in conversation with others. Those who know effective listening are recognized and appreciated in a world that is not always paying attention. We listen to genuinely understand and interpret another's messages, thus conveying value to others in all of our quality relationships. Speaking is power, but listening is wisdom.

The Power of Listening

I stood behind my three-year-old and told him to pick up his room. I received no response. I said, "Ice cream", and he immediately turned around. We select messages according to what captures our attention. Young children who are not listening learn to create nonverbals of "pseudolistening" or "fake listening" to avoid punishment. Ironically they are often disciplined when they are off task and told to "pay attention" (pointing finger included) without being taught the skills to do so! How, indeed do we "pay attention" and live out of the horrible stories of discipline for not participating in a skill we couldn't know to perform?

Effective listening allows us to keep our power. When we miss a message and are briefly absent, we suddenly feel out of the loop of the conversation, discussion, or meeting agenda. We focus so we may feel confident in our power to respond knowing we are present to the message and to the other. Sometimes we recognize obvious distractions of hunger, temperature comfort, thirst, or need to go to the bathroom. We take care of these needs in order to remain focused, but other distractions or behaviors are not so easily recognized. We pay attention to poor listening behavior to change and affect quality of life.

Effective listening creates a cognitive change. We first learn to notice our bad habits through self-talk and work to overcome those behaviors. All instructors have experienced the horrible test results of a learning piece presented, when all students seemed to be listening and no questions were being asked. Unfortunately, many of us want to rush through the learning and "get done" rather than truly focus on responsible levels of listening: understanding, interpreting, analyzing and responding. I visualize the prof and the glassy-eyed students who are virtually wasting both speaker and listener time, simply for the sake of just moving forward. Further, nobody wants to be "that student". Alex repeatedly questioned what others already knew and challenged perspectives – a lot. He spoke more than anyone. Classmates rolled eyes, zipped backpacks, drummed fingers when Alex's hand went into the air with only a minute left of class. We miss opportunity for learning for fear of being Alex and we hold our questions – but at what expense? Our busy world has taught us of being all too time-conscious when we need to take time and fight the inertia of complacency to fulfill our need to truly learn well. We pay attention to what we need in each experience.

Avoiding judgement plays an important role in listening as well. Kirsty taught with me for awhile. Each day at lunch she would complain – and I had such difficulty listening to someone who complained and whined during moments I could be having fun. The unevenness of a table leg was enough to bring her "poor me" lens out and begin her whining. Clearly, the table wobble was more than she could let go of, and my final straw with listening to her negativity. Each day, I began unscrewing the table leg as I sat down just so she would sit with others … it became a game. When she told us she hated frogs, we sent her one from the science lab with a cigarette in its mouth. She retaliated by emptying my entire classroom and office and hiding all I needed. When I finally listened after the chaos of silly mindgames, I heard beneath the voice of whining and heard a woman who'd been picked on throughout life screaming to receive compassion. We listen deeper, to messages behind the words and withhold our judgement. Self-love and conversation teach us to string the beads of our cellular existence with only loving, compassionate, hope-filled energy. Dividing our listening with negative thoughts or *psychological noise* prevents us from hearing the truth being presented. We continue to let go of dissonance in order to be fully aware.

There is no respect in the arrogance of speaking more than listening. In a culture valuing individual success, we learn to self-promote, to get ideas heard, and to keep eyes on us to maintain our power. We forget. We are not paying attention, we are paying with pieces of Self because we are looking for temporary power. Self-promotion is short-lasting and never completed ... an empty fix. We all know the person who speaks too much, seems to "always be right" and, well, looks just plain silly. My classes laugh at the annoyance self-promoters create. We certainly need to avoid being arrogant by centering ourselves in the true place of power – and we send out respect and value with our reliably effective listening. Speakers reciprocate by sending value, respect – and the authoritative power of knowing. We cognitively work to listen more and speak less.

Listening is 50% of the total communication of message ... and so much more. *We notice* when someone *pays attention* to our words, our nonverbal signals, and our emotions. Our world so seldom pays attention. When someone does, we feel important. We feel precious. Knowing our value becomes our power to change our attitude and focus our listening energy. We reciprocate by valuing and listening to others. We give each time we notice. We have gentle power and receive tenfold when others view us as the one who truly cares.

We keep our power each time we refuse patterns or behaviors of poor listening. Perhaps the greatest barrier to effective listening is the gap between words spoken. Wolvin and Coakley's text on listening cites the capability of speaking at 125 words a minute and the capability of listening to be even 500 words a minute. This wait-time is so excruciating if we don't remember kharma and engage in respect of listening. My grandfather spoke slowly, but I listened with remembrance of a man who would teach me how to eat an entire apple, core and all, piece by piece. Additionally, he came in and sat on the couch each and every time I played the piano ... and clapped when I finished. Moving into a loving place brought patience and wisdom as I listened to his elderly speech struggle. We remember to notice the other as we fill gaps of silence with love and compassion rather than distance of thought.

As an undergraduate, I was an actor. Amazingly, the show brought a different reaction each night. The dynamics of the audience were different, so the reciprocation changed. One night could seem so connected with the audience, it seemed I could move a finger just a bit and they would notice. Other evenings I needed to keep psyching up, because the audience wasn't as responsive. When we receive clear feedback from a listener, it improves the dynamics of our speaking/ performing. Recently, I heard of students who were intentionally seated in chairs immediately in front of a boring instructor. As they actively listened with signs of interest, his lecture delivery became more energetic, impassioned and interesting. The students then feigned boredom, and his delivery spiraled down to the previous level. We often forget listeners are responsible for at least 50% of the communicative interaction and need to be mindful of what we are sending. Greg Proops, who frequently appears on the television show "Whose Line is it Anyway", is an excellent stand-up comedian who's very aware of the audience/listener role. He does not hesitate to tell the audience its part in receiving a very strategically set-up joke. Good for him.

Our effort includes listening with the visual stimuli of nonverbal messages as well. Albert Mehrabian, author of *Silent Message*, claims nonverbal cues consist of as much as 93% of a total message. "38% percent of the meaning coming from the vocal, 55% coming from the facial, and only 7% coming from the verbal (as cited in Wolvin and Coakley 170). Wolvin and Coakley, define listening as "the process of receiving, attending to, and assigning meaning to aural and visual stimuli (69). We send visual and aural stimuli of compassion and caring and respect when we look directly into the eyes of others, the mirror to their soul and the reminder of our interconnectedness. Simultaneously, we look away briefly to avoid discomfort of stares as we arrange our bodies to represent our opening up to message. We uncross arms and legs, avoid blocking behaviors and allow our bodies, as instruments, to live out our intent. We are open. We are ready to listen and accept the other. We do not busy ourselves with distraction, we channel our passion toward other with intent to respond appropriately. We smile and are approachable as the charisma of our souls exudes the brilliance of our facial expression and manner of gesture and posture. Authentic, matching verbal and nonverbal signals send messages of respect and kindness. We value the other in our noticing.

Remember the barrier or cost of time? Our time is precious. Research shows we only give speakers ten seconds before we decide to pay attention or tune out. If we are to be effective in our listening power we extend our attention to listen deeper, with our gut. Our gut is our intuition and our intuition is most certainly never wrong. Intuitive listening never serves us poorly. Noticing a message at this level moves us out of complacent listening behavior and into a more active sense of listening and deciding beneath words. Our intuitive sense knows to pay attention – we've simply learned to forget this power.

Authentic power is derived from a blend of Wolvin and Coakley's five levels of listening: discriminative, recreational, informative, therapeutic, and critical and our own ability to move into intuitive lens.

Discriminative Listening

Discriminative listening is our conscious identification of sound. Infants distinguish mother's and father's voices from other voices. Toddlers identify sounds of animals, trains, favorite cartoon characters. Children learn control of the world around them when they can identify sound. One night, my young children and I lay on the bed, listened, and identified the "scary" basement sounds of water heater, furnace, steps upstairs, and plumbing. Being aware of our environments allows us to sense we are safe. Listening in this manner also derives a great deal of sensual pleasure. Years ago I awoke to the sound of loons on a lake and I look forward to my next experience of falling asleep to the rhythm of ocean waves.

A recent trip to the rain forest of Costa Rica provided an overabundance of new sounds to identify while surrounded by monkeys, toucans, and other birds. I heard an ape-like sound as I sat in a hot tub after a mud bath at an outdoor spa. Ironically, the loud sound was caused by very small monkeys above me swinging in the trees. I noticed and remembered the image because of the dissonance – the volume seemed incongruous to the nonverbal cue. We open ourselves to recognizing and paying attention to the harmony of our existence as intrinsic connectedness to the world.

Recreational Listening

Recreational listening allows relaxation and enjoyment while requiring minimal energy to provide us much aesthetic pleasure. We enjoy what is perhaps an otherwise mundane experience of working out, cleaning or commuting. Because the instrumentals create the mood, we are open to listening and/or accepting lyrical messages as well. Gregorian chant allows openness for meditation and steel drums accompany the margarita mood of a Jimmy Buffet concert. Combined images artists create mix with our emotions to create memories for a lifetime. A band member sang Journey's "Open Arms" to me when I was twenty-one. I still sense the essence of that moment when I hear the song and I feel the warmth of his breath in my ear and the slowness of the dance. Music evokes such rich sentiment.

We engage many vehicles of entertainment for the pleasure of our social entertainment and/or listening. Storytelling, theatre, and comedy all create memorable moments with minimal listening effort, thus enabling us to let go and enjoy. We fill ourselves by listening to the soul, the artistry, the creations of others. Truly, *recreational listening* is a gift of beauty and aesthetic moments of serenity in our world of stress and noise.

Comprehensive Listening

Comprehensive listening is a level of listening applied to learning situations where we must integrate knowledge and content. Processing information does not necessitate much brainwork and is an easy level of learning, although we've all heard lectures in the workplace and educational experiences that are challenging to our energy levels because we seem to be receiving no energy or passion from the soul of the speaker. Yellowed notes, the doldrum of frequent powerpoint words, minimal eye contact, weak voice, and nonverbal blocking signals convey discomfort with students or employees, thus confusing clarity of message and creating more effort for the listener. Conversely, I once knew an instructor who loved her job – she believed in her students and exposed them to music, thought, stories, and food of a culture that went far beyond the words of a Spanish textbook. Her animated use of eyes, face, body and voice mood was contagious, and I was moved to goals of speaking Spanish beyond the classroom. Clearly, we sense when a speaker has passion for his/her vocation and for us. A wise speaker clearly states the reason to need the information to raise the level of concern and listening. A wise listener motivates him/her self by creating internal reason or motivation. Sometimes, we simply listen to *do unto others as we would have them do unto us.*

A woman who listens to her Self and understands is doing beautifully for herself. She is moving into acceptance and love in an unconditional manner – accepting human weakness and strength and knowing only love of Self through *understanding*. She allows the gap time between speaking and listening to be used meaningfully toward creating perspective. She allows the other to paint the colors of his/her reality on the canvas of his/her perspective. She gently observes the painting and assumes the virtual reality of the truth of the other. She accepts both the truth of the other and the other.

Masculine and feminine styles of listening differ. Masculine listening involves listening for information and using the information for power. Masculine listening supercedes feminine listening for comprehension. Feminine listening style incorporates a much deeper understanding of information by moving into heart and head together to listen with compassion. Women can assume quiet power of understanding toward all through interconnectedness and wisdom. Interconnectedness becomes our authority of masculine power.

Therapeutic Listening

Therapeutic listening is challenging and rewarding. We choose to take in the discriminatory messages of aural and visual, then we interpret the emotional response as well. If we listen successfully as therapeutic or empathic listeners, we reciprocate with our own compassionate response. Sympathy infers a "feeling sorry for" response--an imbalance of power due to life circumstance. Empathy keeps equality intact, but images what it must truly have felt like to be in a particular situation. The emotion, not the circumstance is the connection. I'm reminded of Atticus Finch in *To Kill a Mockingbird* who modeled non-judgemental listening and equality in relationships throughout the novel as he "walked around in someone else's skin for awhile." The concept of empathy infers we have listened to information, watched nonverbal cues, and chosen an appropriate emotion for response and connection. We take on a heartfelt reception of the message. We value the other and the accompanying vulnerability, thus building trust. Covey remarks:

> ***Empathic listening is so powerful because it gives you accurate data to work with. Instead of protecting your own autobiography and assuming thoughts, feelings, motives and interpretation, you're dealing with the reality inside another person's head and heart. You're listening to understand. You're focused on receiving the deep***

communication of another soul. – Stephen Covey, *Seven Habits of Highly Effective People (1989)*

Fortune 500 companies are taking notice of head and heart listening. An employee bothered by personal problems cannot be productive, happy, or healthy. Leaders in the workforce are answering this need with inclusion and development of appropriate therapeutic listening components. Companies thrive when employees have let go and can find happiness in vocation. Further, these same employees serve others with kindness and openness, improved customer satisfaction, improved productivity, and a desire to remain with the company.

Trust is built when we let go of our concerns by putting them out into a space where we can see them, analyze them, and sort them. Reciprocation of this trust builds the support we need for our Self-confidence. Listening, rather than speaking, allows trust to flow toward the speaker to figure out life situations in a supportive moment. Relationships of this nature are real and bring confidence. Relationships with an intimate other are the building blocks of self-love. Knowing we are *liked* and *trusted* provides a path not only toward self-love, but also toward self-*like*, which sends positive messages to body, mind, spirit.

The over-stimulation of our culture deters connection and valuing of others. We are numbed by a constant barrage of messages and are losing sensitivity to others unless we return to silence. Students are walking around campuses full of lush fragrances of flowers, verdant splendor of greenery and soothing, graceful fountains. They meet others with a richness of culture and ideas and perceptions. And they are missing an integral social piece of college life, because they are numbed to noticing and to the *present*. Technology removes to a different place and isolates from connecting with the world of the present. Cellphones attached to ears of smokers congregating outside campus buildings allow them to puff away to the fog of a different galaxy while humans stand in front of them – unnoticed. We can choose to pay attention.

Empathic listening fulfills the need to be valued or connected because it names our fear of disconnect and loneliness. Loneliness hits all of us as we suffer through broken relationships. Loneliness hits in the midst of all else and in the moments of spring and sunshine when we are expected to find joy. In these moments we realize we want so badly to just fit in and be accepted. We find affirmation to be compassion. The listening other understands and gives value to our thoughts, our fears, our being. When we put aside all else, sit, and give attention through eyes, face, and body, we send silent messages of value. We allow the reality of two souls to touch. When we sit with someone and look into the eyes, the mirror of their soul, we connect with spirit. When we are listened to we are affirmed and propelled into our voice's true path.

Silent and *listen* contain the same letters. Silence is listening. If we are equal, we allow the other to name, sort, and conclude appropriate direction for a problem or situation. Another reality can be refreshing. We all need some "psychological breath" from time to time. I am listened to each Friday morning. A group of women friends and I walk or cross country ski around a lake. We have a variety of vocations: accountant, bus driver, jeweler, florist, financial advisor, teacher – but we are the same in that we are women who need our fun and "psychological breath". We walk, talk, sort, and laugh or cry as we share. A woman has named us "The Joy Walk Club". Indeed, the listening provides freedom for the upcoming weekend and work week, and I'm graced and empowered in the connection and strength of these women.

Women are better empathic listeners. Men and women alike turn to women for compassion, in most cases. Women who understand choose to move into hearts and feel the very essence of the messages, emotions, and the Self is creating love and compassion for Self. Each time women allow feeling and experiencing instead of running from pain, busying to avoid the pain, or numbing to block the pain, they are growing in coping. Women can dare to face the pain. Women can dare to work through the necessary stages of healing, opening up to clarity and letting go of dissonance. A woman who chooses to heal rather than fall victim knows her own power and can take her empathy out to others to create bridges of hope.

Critical Listening

Critical listening is the lens through which we should view our reality as we 1)obtain information, 2)involve empathy and compassion as needed, and 3) sort our response from rational fact and the extension of value system. Critical listening involves much effort or work to efficiently incorporate the aforementioned skills. Women own their authoritative power when they accept and reject messages through experience of their deepest value structure.

In my teaching I incorporate music as an important vehicle of persuasion and clear illustration of critical thought. Our critical thinking is necessary because it has such emotional potential. The mood of the instrumentals can create within us an emotion that is open to the truth of the lyrics. Shared values created by the aural images can create shared sentiment and connect several individuals sharing a similar emotional experience. The cigarette lighters during concerts in the eighties are replaced by mosh pits and bodysurfing today, and both provide historical experience and memory with particular artists and songs as connectedness of a culture. If we do not use critical listening, we are simply taken in by the message – possibly one which does not mesh with our value system. I remember singing the lyrics "I'll be the one to tuck you in at night" by Uncle Kracker awhile ago from his hit song "Follow Me" (*Double Wide,* 2000). My children are the ones who pointed the other lyrics out to me:

I don't care about the ring you wear
Cause as long as no one knows then nobody can care

You're feelin guilty and I'm well aware
But you don't look ashamed and baby I don't care

Hmmmm ... I certainly wasn't meaning to sing a song promoting infidelity – particularly around my children. Conversely, the theme song to one of my favorite television shows, "Scrubs" contains the lyrics:

I can't do this all on my own.
No I won't. I'm no Superman.

These lyrics connect with my truth of vision of knowing we can't live experience on our own; we needn't be Superman. We do "this" human life experience in connection with inner self and relationship with others. Fully present moments of discernment provide lyrics to help us pronounce ourselves. We need to take care by using our critical listening skills. Many of us know the experience of hearing a song for the first time and expressing strong dislike. Some time later, we realize we now like the song – and do not remember changing. When we don't critically listen, we are taken in by the preference to harmony instead of dissonance. We simply subconsciously choose to accept the lyrical or musical message rather than repeatedly fighting the discord. We're easily taken in by messages produced by a billion-dollar industry with geniuses in marketing and we are singing songs outside our Selves and our values. Conscious critical acceptance of listening allows us to experience our true power through the metaphor of music. Imagine how audiences felt hearing Crosby, Stills, Nash and Young perform "Four Dead in Ohio" as the nation mourned the deaths of four college students at Kent State. Powerless, confused students on all campuses experienced emotional truth of the tragedy. Created interconnectedness of authenticity and truth in a song that voiced their mourning and fear. They couldn't run ... because they "knew" what was in their hearts. The song was banned certain places because of its antiwar lyrics – a sacred song expressing heartfelt knowing … a tribute to *life* rather than *killing*. The same culture grasped at Coca Cola messages teaching the world harmony and an image of standing hand-in-hand-- as we fought the Vietnam War. Music is a major part of our history and reality. We find richness and meaning in the music of a culture. As such, it deserves critical listening attention. We pay attention to the musical genre and reality of our existence and value systems.

Critical listeners who act according to values easily work within the missions of the workplace. Critical listeners are leaders who move forward with their learning to change toward moral good with the knowledge and skills they've integrated. Critical listeners are the movers and shakers of our future who engage in civic responsibility, community action, and social movement.

When we don't pay attention, we can be seduced and/or coerced. We should be listening and talking and talking about listening … listening to our feminine power. Our boundaries are challenged and we refuse complacency and inertia. We go within and wake from our numbness. We rest in our intuitive voice and find introspection and examination and satisfaction. We refuse to suffer the insomnia of inappropriate choice. Rather we awake to the authority of our passion and values and move forward strongly, amazingly, confidently toward change, and we are changed.

I listen to Kirsty's whinings in order to be transformed. I listen to the "Joy Walk Club" women affirming my voice in friendship. I learn from both perspectives. A woman who critically listens to Self moves into growth through life experience. She allows the transformation of suffering and joy to move her into a place of wisdom, maturity, and quiet power of knowing. I am transformed remarkably with visions and insights of those who've faced despair and death. People arise with new listening. Each day is gift and each person we encounter is opportunity. We move into gratitude of living with others and interior freedom by means of listening.

Critical listening is the key to our interior freedom. We gently learn understanding and acceptance of and for our Selves and new growing edges. We comprehend the marvelous magnificence of our intricate Being and learn focused attention to messages we choose to lovingly keep within the cognition of our Being. We extend non-judgemental, open understanding and learn our gentleness and patience with Self. We move into deepest empathy and create the therapy of nurturing our existence into good. We dare to feel. We remove the anger of self-deprecating thought and listen to love, compassion, and respect given freely because we choose to know. *Anger does no good.* In our self-love we listen and learn and *do good.* We sort and unpack our life experiences and move out of our complacency deciding to move forward accepting and giving only love and compassion to self, others, and world. And we intuit new form and take shape as catalysts who *do good.* We open our Selves to the grandeur and honor of moving out of a conventional relationship with Self and into post-conventional relationship with Self which is transcendent, glorious, and awesome. Truly, we create our own loveliness as we listen and behold. Open up.

Ephphatha: Be opened. – Mark 7:34

Chapter Four

Sacred Feminine and Quiet Power

"I believe that all of us are created with a sacred emptiness inside. One spiritual writer calls it a 'spaciousness.' The task of spirituality, then, is to keep this spaciousness empty. The temptation is to fill this void with distractions or temporary fixes. Our soulfulness depends on letting go and orienting our deep longings toward the only one who can fill it ... God." – Kevin Anderson

I compare you to a kiss from a rose on the grey. – Seal

Pura Vida is the saying in Costa Rica where ample opportunity exists to experience "Pure Life" of food, nature, fun, and adventure. We enjoyed the essence of *just being* in the splendor of the Rain Forest and the mountains and the ocean – it was unforgettable. My favorite memory is of the day we went to the rain forest and went on the canopy ride hundreds of feet above the ground. Imagine ten to fifteen treehouses with cables connecting them that form a path downward just above the canopy of the rainforest and all it's exotic beauty. I befriended the guide during our hike up and I savored the challenge of speaking Spanish with him. The group was unaware of our conversation, and so it came as a surprise when I announced what he'd convinced me to do – which was to slide down the cable hanging upside down in tandem with his cable seat. I looked at my husband, who is an engineer and understands cable, and he agreed it would be safe. I then hooked my cable to the guide's, wrapped my legs around his waist and flipped backwards and upside down while we slid over the canopy. If you knew how timid my truest nature is you'd understand just how surprisingly free I felt letting go of all of my fears and reservations and simply enjoying the thrill.

Pura vida for me is the time I let go literally and figuratively to find joy. Our spirit is yearning so much for us to let go, trust, and find joy. It's scary to do so, because we move out of our comfort zone or need to control our environment, but the result of practice through contemplative listening brings the most amazing joy and love we can ever dream to know. Happiness is formed from within, and every time we let go of an Ego-based deception, we become more vividly the woman waiting to announce her voice and place in life. The last four years of my life have been so remarkable, I can no longer keep the beauty to myself. I desire all women to *know* unconditional love and acceptance, because I have a vision of grand connectedness and power of feminine voice: where all is possible and world healing is possible. Experience the remarkable nature of true voice waiting to announce itself to others.

Jack Keroac had a vision when he wrote *On the Road* in 1952 and completely changed the nation. The book named the fear of complacency the younger generation felt while growing up in the unrest of nuclear anxiety. Underneath the image of June Cleaver cutting vegetables in her kitchen at the "Leave it to Beaver" household, was a nagging voice echoing "Is this all there is?" Keroac showed a life engulfed with passion and pleasure and spiritual awakening. Even the style of his writing was free from the restrictions and rules of grammar. Keroac preferred to write about snapshot moments of intense, sensual living where "tires kissed the highway" and left the perceived reality of establishment and control. The artistic genius of: Ken Kesey, author of *One Flew Over the Cuckoo's Nest*; Jerry Garcia, "The Grateful Dead"; Neal Cassady, symbol of hope and change (Dean

Moriarity in Keroac's novel) and many others collectively formed the Merry Pranksters, who took a bus trip in a bus called "Furthur" to connect a nation. Specifically, the bus went from Californinia to New York to visit LSD guru Timothy Leary for "Spiritual Discovery" (Searles, 1991). Symbolically, the combined artistry of the Pranksters and followers spread a message of a truth with no limits. The nation was forced to take notice. Cassady and Keroac challenged bureaucracy and establishment systems by creating a counterculture that simply wanted more than complacency. Keroac's writing was analyzed for its rhetorical or communicative value by Omar Swartz's article "Rhetorical Transformation in Kerouac's *On the Road.*" Swartz identifies Keroac's symbolic naming of unrest as created by the Beat culture. Swartz writes how Keroac "empowers people to take control of their lives and to reject the dominant forces that constrain their thoughts and their actions". As the flame that ignited the Beatnik movement and hippie counterculture, Keroac moved a nation out of their heads and into their hearts. Keroac guided from Conventional to Post-conventional value because he saw his truth and lived it. Keroac experienced his truth by paying attention to spirit. Specifically, he removed ego and followed spiritual bliss through three connotations of "beat". "Beat" is 1.) the rhythm or breath of life, 2.) as defined in a public discussion by Holmes (as cited in Swartz):

> ***More than mere weariness, it implies the feeling of having been used, of being raw. It involves a sort of nakedness of mind, and ultimately, of soul; a feeling of being reduced to the bedrock of consciousness. In short, it means being undramatically pushed up against the wall of oneself.***

Finally, "Beat" becomes a Catholic, spiritual connotation for a religious experience. "It meant 'beatitude,' a Catholic condition of blessedness." (Sorrell, 1982 as cited in Swartz).

Our culture is complacent in its busyness. We have moved back into our head, and our ego, and our conventional thinking about material value. Our hearts scream for focus as they burn out from fragmented passion. They are longing for interconnectedness. We keep trying to *do* to fill the need we have, and we've become pieces rather than whole. We need to stop *doing* and start *being*. We need to channel our passions toward spirit, passion, and compassion, toward our own "condition of blessedness". We *know* this is not all there is. We know there is "something there" to be gently guided into and know our place. We push ourselves against the wall of our very Self and dare question what we need. We engage in life meaningfully, writing our own novels from the pages and experiences so richly creating our own path of truth. We know this in our experiential knowing, our Highest Good.

> ***The roots of contemporary spirituality are to be found in an emphasis on human experience. In all its variety and pain, our ordinary human experience becomes the immediate context for God's self-disclosure.***
>
> – Philip Sheldrake, *Spirituality and Theology (1999)*

We constantly need to sort the truth from within, our deepest knowing, to resolve the conflict with a dissonant world. The obstacle on our spiritual path is the reality created by the establishment. Establishments keep structure and order rather than chaos. Establishments are necessary, but we have a right to question. In our busyness, we are complacent to questioning and we are moved forward blindly and powerfully-- losing freedom, values, voice and right to be true to our Selves. The acid and LSD of the counterculture provided a means to remove barriers in thinking, allowing the boundaries of rational to no longer restrict the *beyond rational*, or creative. The *beyond rational* is the sensual, the creative, the part to our selves that begs to be noticed and fulfilled. Our *spirit* removes the barrier of complacency to refocus our creativity into a focused world where there is bliss. Our bliss guides us to notice the interconnectedness of our mystical experience. Our feminine spirit and energy can heal an entire world and guide others to bliss as we all create the symbolic novels that write the path toward world good.

The Rose on the Grey

Shopping at high-end boutiques, indulging in a chocolate martini or a mojito and inhaling an entire rack of Kansas City ribs, or joining friends for a frothy beer in the sun provides sensual pleasure and fun. Knowing appropriate boundaries allows us to continue to savor fun throughout life, though it's a lifelong discernment to gain perspective of when we are engaging in pleasure and when we are deceiving ourselves into consequences of overindulgence and/or unhealth. People who find life dull or grey have lost clarity. Clarity of vision provides appropriate channeling of energy and passion. Human experience is distracted from clarity by leading to perceived needs or addictions. The false roses of addictions slowly move in and manipulate the rational self. We enjoy a sensual pleasure and we want to experience it again. Slowly, we begin deceiving ourselves into more and more of the pleasure, until life is so grey without, we have convinced our brain to need the pleasure. The self-deception grows with addiction until it controls our thinking. Only when we empty ourselves of addictions can there be room to be filled. Our *beyond rational* noticing fills us with healing. When we are healed, we *savor* the sensual pleasures of life, but we no longer *need* the pleasure. Rolheiser says if we allow our passions to keep being filled by other pieces, such as material wealth, knowledge, addictions, we never are emptied to fill our Selves with the *true longing of needing to be loved.* To be in touch with spirit is to fill ourselves with power, voice and possibility. The true "rose on the grey" is our personal relationship and connectedness to the "something there" that is Divine Power or energy and our interconnectedness to all. We breathe into the rhythm of life.

Each time we meditate or pray, we leave ego behind. Ego is a perceived reality of comparison and competition of materialism. Further, our ego finds power in control, not letting go. Our ego is our safety, our rational, and we are threatened so we latch on to systems of control, creating a downward spiral and distancing from inner connectedness. Systems can also drain us and I felt drained of energy from giving to others – beat. Mary and I floated on innertubes on Lake Sylvia, drinking in coolness and conversation as intermingled with lapping waves and hot sun that swallowed my words of doubt and fear. I let go as ego dripped into the water and was carried out to an island of isolation. Letting go fills our spirit. Moving into the *beyond rational* of our experience allows us to return to a rational world with connected, loving vision. We live a condition of blessedness.

Living life engaged with passion gives meaningful countenance of self to others. Quiet power affects others and the world. Dalai Lama's book, *How to Practice: The Way to a Meaningful Life* focuses on moving away from harming others. Only egos wish to harm continuing deceived need to compare and compete. Our spirit knows only the condition of love. The Dalai Lama states:

> ***The morality of concern for others – called the morality of Bodhisattvas (being primarily concerned with helping others) – is mainly practiced by restraining the mind from falling into selfishness. For those practicing Bodhisattva morality, the essential point is to refrain from self-cherishing, but also to refrain from ill deeds of body and speech***.– The Dalai Lama, *How to Practice: The Way to a Meaningful Life*

Our decisions become extensions of our goodness. Our sacred bodies magnificently extend our values and unconditional love to others. To live a life with no limits of human potential, no limitations, no boundaries to the beauty of what our true selves can create is to live life boldly, intensely, passionately, miraculously. When we begin noticing the spiritual aspect of self we have clarity of vision and are open to the graces and gifts and beauty of our experiences.

We cannot feel Supreme Being or energy in the **future**, so we need to stay in the **present**. If we fill ourselves with worrying, we are in the future and lose our spiritual power. Remember, *worry* is derived from a word meaning "divided energy". Ego believes worrying protects us. In worry and fear, we are half our potential. In our meditation and prayer, we come to discover present wholeness. What if there were nothing to be afraid of? What if we can really be amazing? What if moving into our true selves really bought joy, fulfillment, and concern for others? Well, then, the world would be changed, wouldn't it?

We move into honest self-love. We examine in silence the confusion of self-doubt, shame, and regret. We evoke our interior freedom. In our silence of sorting we can learn to **let go** of the weight and concern and move into a place of self-love. We love ourselves every day in the silence. Women flow with a cycle and rhythm that touches our intuition, our relationships, and our world as we are meant to be. We are meant to love and be loved. Mother Teresa's Nobel Peace Prize acceptance speech contains the word "love" 56 times. Clearly, she knew of the Catholic condition of blessedness in order to speak with such grand love in her human experience.

Contemplative Listening

We take pleasure in connection with "something there" in our ecstatic silence. The definition of "something there" is individually unique and precious. Humans have an inherent desire to connect with something grander. Contemplative listening flutters as a sacred space of awareness warming my solar plexis, rising into my heart, igniting a way to know life's meaning. Maureen Conroy, R.S.M, author of *Looking into the Well* defines contemplative listening as a "reverent attentiveness" and we view the more that is life. The cool stuff of epiphanies and "aha" moments point the next step. We live lives of conflict resolution as we discern dissonance within self; with others; and place in the world. Contemplative listening resolves or heals conflict in a transcendent manner; we discern life decisions and barriers in the presence of our spirit. Our reverent attentiveness interweaves clarity to eloquently move into freedom of knowing next step of spiritual path. Each and every time we evoke our spirit, healing replaces conflict. Dissonance moves into resolution and wholeness: creating new narratives of calm. A vessel of longing is filled with the gift of interior freedom and perception of spiritual power, feminine power.

We experience conditions of blessedness.

Blessedness is an experiential grace for diverse religious audience. I envision the interconnectedness and definitions of divine providing grace according to individual need. All who listen experience beauty of transformation amidst those times when life is hard. Divine intricately designs meaningful moments – so we may be touched in just the right way. Contemplative listening brings others to a serendipitous weaving of souls in a symphony, a condition of blessedness touching each soul gently, exactly as needed. Gray Matthews, Ph.D, University of Memphis, eloquently writes of contemplative listening as a forerunner in communication theory. He urges all to notice and move beyond current communication excellence to a transcendent relationship or communion (18) with the other. Communing and beholding the other as spirit is grace each and every time.

Contemplation is literally derived from the Latin *con*, which means "intensive" and *templum* which is a place to look. As we move into contemplative listening, we take an intense look at our life from a space, or *beyond rational* place that allows for time restrictions and interruptions of thought to fade away. In that space we take a long look at our life experiences, our relationships, our vocations to "see" our lives from a transcendent lens. In this space we are given permission to let go of our concerns and rest in peace. Giving this continued attention and focus allows us to move into our true self and quiet power. This deeper knowing allows our lives to be touched like the soft beauty of the "kiss of a rose". We listen beyond words in silence from a space that intuits the "more" we search for with our most passionate desires, and, in fact, even allows us to experience the veil that exists between knowledge and experience, words and silence, rational and beyond rational. Christians recognize the biblical phrase, "Be still and know that I am God." God comes to us in the silence.

The Dalai Lama describes meditation similarly:

> ***Subjective meditation [is] your aim to cultivate in the mind a new, or strengthened perspective or attitude. The cultivation of faith is an example of this type of meditation; faith is not the object on which you are concentrating but an attitude that is being meditatively cultivated.***
>
> – The Dalai Lama, *How to Practice: The Way to a Meaningful Life*

Both prayer and meditation bring us back to our morality and our love in moments of silence. Wisdom is achieved in silence. Thomas Merton was a Trappist Monk, writer, and peace and civil rights activist. He knew a lens of interconnectedness:

> ***It is in deep solitude that I find the gentleness with which I can truly love my brothers. The more solitary I am, the more affection I have for them. It is pure affection and filled with reverence for the solitude of others.*** – Thomas Merton, *A Year With Thomas Merton: Daily Meditations from His Journals*

College students engaged in a listening unit on contemplative listening, and journaled to notice some of their experiences. One student painted a definition of contemplative listening with a quotation from Ray Bradbury:

> ***The wind sighed over his shelled ears. The world slipped bright over the grassy rounds of his eyeballs like images sparked in a crystal sphere. Flowers were suns and fiery spots of sky strewn through the woodland. Birds flickered like skipped stones across the vast inverted pond of heaven. His breath raked over his teeth, going in ice, coming out fire. Insects shocked the air with electric clearness. Ten thousand individual hairs grew a millionth of an inch on his head. He heard the twin hearts beating in his throat beating in each ear, the third beating in his throat, the two hearts throbbing his wrists, the real heart pounding his chest. The million pores on his body opened. I'm really alive! He thought. I never knew it before, or if I did I don't remember!*** – Ray Bradbury, *Dandelion Wine*

The clarity of this moment is a spiritual noticing. Nature brings all a sense of the "bigger than" human experiences which are our connectedness to world energy, Supreme Being, Truth. Meditation and prayer bring clarity and awareness of just being. College students in my course engaged in Contemplative Listening for one hour a week throughout the course, and reflected on "just being" in spirit. The insights gained while communing with Self/God in silence are authentic and pure.

One student experienced a moment of serendipity: "Your heart is pure, your mind clear, and your soul devout." This fortune came from a fortune cookie, the first thing eaten after a Muslim student fasted for Ramadan. The student was meditating with a contemplative listening exercise presenting reverent attention to the fortune presented in the cookie. He listened deeper and saw his holiness and connection with Allah. Amazing. He added:

> ***Throughout the semester I tried to listen to myself in various ways: through the prayer, by taking long walks through the forest, listening [to] music, etc. All of the exercises that I tried were very valuable and very effective; I have to admit: it is pretty amazing how one can change only if one is opened to admitting and accepting mistakes.***

Spiritual Self experiences healing in moments of sorting and experiencing as exemplified in this powerful example:

> ***Often I noticed that my body was telling me to slow down, take a breath, and not sweat the small stuff. Interesting to note as well, I found that while at first I always felt spiritually "neutral" or "okay," by the end of the reflection I was always feeling more philosophic as my mind worked to answer life's tough questions and sort chaos into order. While I never discovered the meaning to life, I did discover that taking time for intrapersonal reflection and myself is extremely important for me as a perfectionist who needs time to unwind.***

Another student spoke of the calming effect Self receives from Christian perspective:

> ***Prior to this class I understood self-listening to be myself when I am praying and I still believe this. ... Often times when the world around us puts pressure and stressors on us we can suppress emotions and feelings inside us so deep we aren't aware that they are there, and often times in need of nurturing. This aspect of self-listening is my biggest weakness; I can pray twice daily and sometimes fail to acknowledge my emotions/feelings. I became aware***

> ***of this weakness only recently when my family and I were going through a challenging time. … Through this difficult time all my family and I knew how to do was pray. It wasn't until our first journal entry in this class that I took time for myself to reflect on the previous week and it was then that I became aware of how I forgot about my fears and all the weakness I forced aside. As I sat quietly in my room I became aware of all the anxiety and fear I had felt but kept hidden during the previous week. I actually started to tear up just thinking about how I could pray so intensely [for my family] but forgot to thank God for all of the gifts He has given me through [my family]. I had never been aware of prayer working where I wasn't true to my own emotions and feelings. I was hiding from them until now.***

Personal relationship with Self, over time, is catalyst of change and growth – especially in epiphany of transformation:

> ***Until recently, one of my greatest weaknesses has been intrapersonal listening. I had been in this terrible relationship with John for about a year. … Then we started keeping listening journals for this class. The lectio activity was so beneficial. I heard songs on the radio all of the time that made me want to cry every time I heard them. After we did the lectio in class, I began doing it on my own and keeping track of the songs and how they made me feel. About two weeks ago, I read through all my lectios, and found a common theme. You guessed it, John. As I actually read the words in front of me which described in painful detail how much emotional stress he had caused***

me, I came to a conclusion. This had to stop, and I was the only one who could put an end to it. So I ended it right there. I don't think about him like that anymore and when I hear our songs, they just remind me of a time in my past. While I have moved on, those memories will always be with me, but they will no longer plague my every waking moment. Since that day, I have felt like a tremendous weight has been lifted off my shoulders, and I can be me again. I have even found that listening to myself has become so much easier than I had ever imagined it could be. Eliminating that pain from my life has also made me a better interpersonal listener because I can really hear and feel the problems my friends are having, without pulling the "John cloud" in with me.

Spiritual Direction

Contemplative Listening can also come in silence and presence of a spiritual director, or guide to journey in personal relationship with divine. We learn about ourselves when we make connections to what is true – sometimes we need the aid of another presence to do so. We struggle in silence, alone with our thoughts and selves – this can be challenging, but it can also become beautifully familiar as we grow in self-acceptance and love. We remove our thinking and move out of our heads and into the passion and compassion of our hearts. If we meditate, we allow the silence to speak and bring us to acceptance and oneness. If we pray, we speak genuinely and openly. And … the most important part … we *listen back.* We listen for response, nudging, noticing. Sometimes the response is not in our time, but God's time, and when we least expect it. Katherine Kraft, O.S.B. once spoke about prayer. She asked us to imagine our favorite love song. She asked us to sing the song to God as a form of prayer. Then she asked us to *listen back* as God sang it back. Wow--such grand love.

As spiritual director, I guide the breath of Holy Spirit within me, as vessel, resonating with swirls of interconnected breath and life as I savor the journey of another discerning life path. I savor experiences of knowing silent connection in contemplative awareness ... watching another come to moments of breathing the rhythm of life and condition of blessedness. A symphony of interconnectedness follows each sorting of life experience in a fully present moment of harmony, balance and silence. The other meaningfully comes to what divine intends and is shaped from a sacred space within. I am graced with watching others fully embrace life meaningfullly – experientially. The other, called the "directee" does the work of changing and listening to come to next place of authenticity. There is no turning back from the reverence of these sessions. We are both forever preciously changed.

I am the midwife as women give birth to their souls and True Beings:

> ***The midwife enters the lost places with her who will give birth. The midwife is the women-between: the liminal woman, the threshold woman. She focuses her energy upon the coming through. Coming through birth. Coming through dis-ease. Coming through death. She keeps us breathing, keeps us one with the universal rhythm of creation. She sings the song of breath, turning our fear and the frenetic struggle resulting from it into an intricate dance of becoming*** – Weber, *Blessings*

Each and every time I meet with another, I guide his/her spirit: but the receiving is twofold. I **always** receive the grace of experiencing divine as the other sorts life experience. Spiritual direction is a precious part of my being, my soul, my passion. It is the root base of every single other part of my life, it creates the lens of seeing all I experience and discern as I move through human experience. What spiritual direction is not, is counseling, but it's sometimes used in parallel manner. As we come to authenticity, we sometimes find issues needing advice with psychological professionals, especially when dealing with anxiety or depression. The focus of spiritual direction is intended for all spirits who desire to know Supreme Being. Carolyn Myss speaks of the distinct difference between suffering in life experience or the longing of spiritual desire.

Clearly, the distinction between a clinical depression and a spiritual crisis can sometimes be a fine line. Another way of recognizing it is to observe the way you respond to a crisis. If you react by asking yourself how you will ever find someone to replace your divorced spouse or lost loved one, how you can get out of a job that's killing you, or how you can find enough money to live, more than likely your depression is primarily psychological. If you respond specifically to the feeling of having been rendered powerless by being consumed with anger, resentment, or blame directed toward others, you are most likely not spiritually depressed. (When in doubt, of course, you should always consult your physician or a mental health professional.) If, however, you are asking yourself questions about the meaning of life or about why God seems so distant from you, then most likely you're in a spiritual crisis, and you may need to seek out a spiritual director rather than a psychotherapist. – Carolyn Myss, *Sacred Contracts*

Spiritual directors commune with others in affirmation and celebration as well. Spiritual Directors listen with the deepest level of transcendence as individuals sort life experience and facts and move into the emotional realm. The director beholds spirit through a process of spiritual unpacking, sorting and listening, frequently noticing or intuiting divine presence. Verbalizing an experience can't do justice to the awesomeness of *knowing our value* at such an incredible level.

To know love and personal relationship in a transcendent belief or faith is everything we need to satisfy our yearning, and yet the desire is lifelong. And those who choose religion learn to embrace sacred text and structure with experiential lens. Once we *know*, we cannot go back to ego and its emptiness. Spiritual Direction is a confidential, individual relationship with someone who is a vessel through whom spirit can "work" or "nudge". As such, it is a passive experience, however; the noticing of spirit within becomes a most active, grace-filled experience. Spiritual reverence and beholding exist when a being opens as vessel for Spirit to work through in just the manner intended. As such, the spirit of God empowers the individual to sort and unpack life experience in terms of personal relationship with connectedness to Supreme Being or energy from non-denominational perspective.

The director guides by listening from the heart and noticing movements of the spirit. There is no advice given, since reverence is given for the individual to come to what is meant for the soul to come to in the experience. Over time, the divine nature of the relationship allows for spiritual growth, freedom, empowerment, and an interdependent view of the world.

I was immersed in a community of unconditional love with the nuns at the St. Benedict Monastery who were my teachers, my classmates, my environment, and my grace in life. The Benedictine (Catholic) Rule "Listening with the Ear of the Heart" is the precious base of the experience, although it is respectfully taken to others in a non-denominational manner. I came into the program very much a person "of the world" and from a far different culture than the community. I received only love and acceptance. I'd never met nuns before, and it was peculiar how I could be myself in a place I expected would hold more judgment than the reality of my personal life. Instead, I found no judgment, and I needed no image. I found relief.

Through the rigor of the studying and interning I experienced the grandest view of connectedness formed from the relationship of myself and my directees, spiritual director, peer supervisors and teachers. Indeed, spiritual experiences cannot be verbalized well, they must be lived. Unspoken, silent awesomeness.

Nudgings and Serendipity

Contemplative listening teaches us to notice nudgings, coincidences, patterns and responses that become the unique gift of our spiritual connection and ultimate joy. We learn that the coincidences of our serendipitous moments are graces and mystical interconnectedness to others and the Higher Good. We dare experience and savor ultimate joy in *beyond rational* experience as the guide for our human experience.

When I met Elizabeth, I knew *communion* immediately. She put the wind back into my sails – literally and figuratively. I was searching for sailing lessons for my husband and was finding little opportunity in our area. As I was playing piano and feeling the essence of my mother in her favorite song "The Flowers of Spring", the phone rang.

"My name is Elizabeth and I know sailing. In fact, I've sailed the ocean." The conversation proceeded and we agreed to three lessons for my husband – what had seemed only minutes ago to be impossible was suddenly remarkably simple and available. I returned to "Flowers of Spring" only to be interrupted by the phone a moment later. Elizabeth asked permission to include my sons as well – even a better gift than I'd thought of! "Flowers of Spring" continued and I received the most beautiful flicker. Mystical experiences are often flickers and feelings of butterfly wings – so brief our hearts know what our mind does not quite know. In this moment, a deep loving feeling came over me. My deceased mother was loving my husband so deeply for taking care of me and loving me all of these years through the gift of Elizabeth – in an instant I *knew* this. My rational thought makes sense of this heartfelt experience as mystical because it interrupted my own thought. Further, rational thought would experience her love for me – to experience her grand love for *him* ... a loving surprise can only be described as *beyond rational* thought. Elizabeth taught my family to keep wind in the sails while sailing. Additionally, Elizabeth and I remain remarkably connected through love of sailing, kayaking, writing, music, and spiritual thought. Truly, Elizabeth's spiritually keeps the wind in my sails as I write for women.

Life is abundant with experiences and graces of personal relationship with God. He/she provides so beautifully in *just the right way*. I only notice the beauty in the silence, but I can hold that whenever I desire and I can be held by the divine whenever I desire. To be clear, it's a fun way to dance through life.

In our silence we know there is something greater which is our very connection to the soul of who we are to be. In this understanding, we no longer need to "fit in", we appreciate our unique place in the world. In our silence we come to understanding and confidence and connection with Self, with Higher Good or energy, and with the interdependent relationship we can have with the world of women's spiritual healing and voice. Ironically, we find our "fitting in" with interconnectedness.

I experience such strong images of my God. In the "aha" moments of my spiritual oneness I see God as a variety of loving images: Male and Female; Mother/Father; Friend; Lover because intuitive senses bring the *intangible* to a transcendent, almost *tangible* place. The images can be called upon when I am suffering, thus offering strong emotional connection. Truly, in the moments of connection with the Divine, we sometimes sense a presence *beyond rational* where there is love. The knowing brings happiness, ecstasy, and joy to human experience.

My soul is needing to be more than self, needing to touch the world and offer voice to the vision of women who blessedly love unconditionally. My soul envisions women living life viewed through the lens of spirit and truth – as "roses on the grey" of a world desperately needing love.

Contemplative Listening for World Healing

Compassion and contemplative listening are a necessary bridge to hope in our culture. A newspaper entitled *Streetwise* in Washington D.C. is successfully connecting social classes with articles of hope from business people who teach struggling citizens finance and how to find jobs and homes. *Streetwise* illustrates the power and energy of our compassion. Struggling victims reciprocate connection and hope as they provide their stories to the business culture. The two cultures are listening ... remarkably listening. The two cultures are paying attention and beholding the experience of the other. *Streetwise* illustrates the possibility of change through focused passion and compassion. Empathy with one being creates understanding and knowing. Soon we intuit possibility. All is possible for our world through the flicker of our hearts which ignite the power of our compassion simply because we pay attention.

Eve Ensler is paying attention. For my fortieth birthday I flew to New York City to see *Vagina Monologues*. It was lifechanging to see and experience such an intense experience of women and women's stories. Eve Ensler is moving women forward on a national level with the V-day Project. Eve Ensler knows her truth and voice and spirit.

Marie Wilson, author of *Phenomenal Woman* is paying attention to feminine truth. Women own quiet power, and the energy of this power is being called forth to heal the violence, fighting, and destruction of spirit in our world. Marie is changing our culture's perception of women in politics.. Marie is teaming up with Eve Ensler with their creation of "Women Elect the Future". The limitless power created in the truth of these women is astounding. I had the pleasure of hearing Marie Wilson speak at a business luncheon. Marie says women know cooperation. All mothers teach siblings to solve conflict and cooperate in the experience of mothering. It's the very concept of connecting through conflict resolution that is so greatly needed on a global scale at this time.

Streetwise, Ensler and Wilson, and all women who dare announce themselves intentionally to the world provide hope and significant change through their passion and wholeness. Connection with spirit within creates interconnectedness with others and world in fully present manner of power. Possibilities are limitless.

> ***Both giant capitalism and state-run bureaucratic socialism suffer from the same lack of Eros – or nearness, of feeling, of care and intimacy with the unemployed and the employed as well as with earth, waters, air, plants, animals, bodies. It is true that Eros is in a special way 'woman's power,' as Lorde puts it, then feminism will furnish a powerful healing to the new civilization we are called to create.***
>
> – Matthew Fox, *Original Blessing*.

Women become mothers who intuitively guide toward connectedness and love. Hilary Clinton gave a speech in China comparing the women/mothers of the culture of our world as pieces in a patchwork quilt. Women's voice is the quiet power of the thread of connectedness in the quilt that will cradle the pain and suffering of our world in arms of divine love.

> ***I know for us compulsive, productive extroverted types, this [silence] is a tall order. The bottom line is – it's worth it. But we have to believe that it really matters. In our culture, silence & stillness have been equated with wasting time, doing nothing, being lazy. NOT TRUE. Think of***

it this way – the silence of meditation is not the silence of a graveyard; it is the silence of a garden growing.
– Linda Douty

Knowledge is learning one new thing each day, but wisdom is letting go of one new thing everyday. – Zen

Chapter Five

The Abundance of Loving Others

Some events and relationships will enchant us and others will crack us wide open with pain. – Carolyn Myss

A woman stands in the sapphire background of the crisp autumn flames of color and watches the brisk air turn her words and breath into vision and smoky essence of vulnerability. She expresses her naked thought and offers a piece of her heart forward. The heartfelt words swirl and smolder in pallid smoke and dissipate – no longer connected to her or to him. He responds with puffs of hurt and anger and memory allowing the pieces of her heart to shatter in the frost of the frozen ground. She stands in her disconnect balancing harmony of self and harmony with other and chooses. The sand on stone grinds as the heel of her boot turns and determinedly creates distance. A leaf falls, unnoticed.

Fulfilling Self Needs in Relationship with Others

Feminine power lies in solitude, but not isolation from others. Our attitude and inherent being looks to connect with others who fulfill us, complete us. We look to others to learn about the truth and virtual reality of our human experience. We share our vision, and receive the visions of others, creating deeper perceptions in connection of ideas. Sometimes our significant others and quality relationships don't understand our choices in friends because they meet different parts of our nature. George, a character on the *Seinfeld* show spoke of "worlds colliding" when different friends, or nuances of his complex nature happened to meet. I have friendships formed for all of my interests: shopping for white, summer linen shirts, trendy purses, and high heels; watching artistic, intellectual films; watching mindless, ridiculously fun films; dancing; yoga; and waterskiing/boating. Have you ever brought all of your friends together for a party or social opportunity only to see them not "get" each other? We are complicated, unique beings with diverse needs. As we create the contours of pronouncing ourselves, we also learn how to announce our true voice to others.

Intellectual needs. I read obsessively and most enjoy authors who write of different perspective who dare to stand out differently. Authors who view the world in similar manner are like my friends, and I can't wait to spend time with them. Further, authors who frame controversy or challenge intellect intrigue me and I am so grateful they pronounce themselves to the world, daring all of us to search deep within and evoke our deepest value formations to know what we are transcendentally made of … they evoke process of discernment and inner freedom. I love discovering others who appreciate same authors and musical artists simply because they share a glimpse of my experiences. I've always bonded with students who share musical interests, as if we "get each other" even when our ages and life experience are so very different. Somehow, the connection builds as a cornerstone to connect understanding in course subject matter as well. Intellectual conversation and challenge keep us growing as lifelong learners. As we age, we tend to allow our experiences to close our mind. Those who open us up to challenge and vision of new possibilities and perceptions engage us in new passion for life experience.

College students engage in conversation with peers for study purposes. Additionally, they seek friendships with students in the same major, and coworkers/mentors for future experience. The ephiphanies of these remarkable experiences often create and ignite the passion of future thought, research, products, and direction.

Intellectual connection is engaging and challenging. Harmless flirtations and nuances of ambiguous phrases connect two intellectually while suggesting a desire for further emotional and physical bonding. Flirtations and private jokes mirror understanding of another with the brief flicker of a glance, playfully connecting.

Emotional needs. Fun is my number one priority and what I look for in others. Clever humor and ambiguity create laughter, relaxation, and release of stress to maintain emotional well-being. We laugh openly with those we trust. We build trusting relationships with others who allow us to be vulnerable while valuing our dignity in their perspective. Years ago I spoke with Diane at a very large party. While we conversed, I picked up a sizeable crumb from the cakepan next to me and ate it – it was awful! "Ick!," I said.

"I made that," she replied.

Imagine my embarrassment. To save her dignity, I added, "I'm so sorry. I thought it was going to be chocolate, and when it wasn't…"

"It *is* chocolate."

Oops. Nowhere to go after that one. My faux paus created a private joke she and I shared for quite some time, as I repeatedly asked her for that recipe … which pointed out my momentary stupidity rather than her error.

We value the dignity of our being, our face. We look to others to "save face" of our dignity amidst daily experiences and actions. Our faces are vulnerable to dynamics during communicative situations. We all fear rejection or failure, what Eastern philosophy calls "losing face." When we communicate well, our face is improved. Awkward or embarrassing moments put us "out of face." We look to fill our emotional needs with those who reciprocate "Facework", the verbal and nonverbal behavior display while communicating in various situations (Goffman, 1971). Those who risk being vulnerable in order to restore our face send nonverbal messages of commitment to our worth. Goffman states, "'poise' is the ability to control emotional reactions and continue to interact even when one's face has been questioned by others as inappropriate or undeserved (Goffman 1967). What about times we are "out of face" and need our image restored?

I remember being out of face a few years back. I was waiting for a few students to finish writing notes, I asked, "Does anyone have a good joke while we're waiting?" A female proceeded to tell a joke most appropriately heard in a bar and it was clearly degrading to women. I remember the awkward moment of quiet and the students watching my face and reaction. They, too, were out of face. A gentleman spoke up, "I think she meant more of a joke like this..." He then proceeded to tell an appropriate, lighter joke, thus restoring the "face" of everyone in the classroom. He had social grace. Trust is built in the vulnerable moments of our emotional selves. We look to those who commit to the poise of guiding us smoothly over awkward moments. Quality friendships are built with solid rocks of trust and those who stand up for us become our anchors.

Dancing through life with social grace is our success since we define ourselves clearly through our relationships with others. When I was forty, we built a house and I spent many hours doing yardwork in the privacy of my backyard. I bought a bikini to enjoy the sun while doing so – and my closest friend bought me a matching necklace which further affirmed and defined my perspective. Consider the gifts of friendship and the depth of meaning behind those who know us well enough to determine exactly how and what to give. Kelly, a student, created suggestions for a figurative c-d to go along with the chapters of this book – and I get tears each time I remember the beauty of her incredible thoughtfulness. Healthy relationships build in intimacy with gradual exchanges of vulnerable or intimate conversation. The other responds with equal sharing, and there is harmony or balance in the relationship. The gift of exchange is twofold: relationships and life are confusing, and it's a relief to lift the weight of our chaos with someone in confidence; and when someone reciprocates the sharing we are valued as beings who are trusted. We revere the other when we genuinely understand and are understood.

We've all experienced the pain of betrayal, but we react and heal differently. When we listen to our hearts and move into understanding or transformation in the pain, we move into healing and loving perspective. We are surrounded by a great many who hold the pain as if they cannot move on. Sadly, their spirit, emotion and physical being conveys the bitterness. Most people are kind, so we search to connect with those deserving of our trust, wearing our hearts openly. We remove ourselves from imbalanced, or shallow relationships that lack trust, so that we may be filled in order to send only our goodness out to others. We do unto others as we would have them do unto us, and we live in awareness of noticing *how* they are doing to us. When those values are reciprocated, we fill an emotional need. We dare continue to need others, rather than live isolated or lonely and find remarkable affection and love: experiences of life's true joy.

Deborah Tannen, Communication theorist and linguist states:

> ***[Porcupines] huddle together for warmth, but their sharp quills prick each other, so they pull away. But then they get cold. They have to keep adjusting their closeness and distance to keep from freezing and from getting pricked by their fellow porcupines – the source of both comfort and pain.***
>
> ***We need to get close to each other to have a sense of community, to feel we're not alone in the world. But we need to keep our distance from each other to preserve our***

> ***independence, so others don't impose on or engulf us. This duality reflects the human condition. We are individual and social creatures. We need other people to survive, but we want to survive as individuals.***
>
> – Deborah Tannen, *That's Not What I Meant*

We live in conflicting needs of self: healing emotional pain caused by others, and needing to look to others for comfort and support. A contemplative life allows us to discern each need in our quiet countenance, especially as we look to fulfill our physical needs maintaining and extending the dignity of our physicality.

Physical Needs. A premature baby in a hospital is touched with the finger of it's parent and responds to treatments to develop. A toddler's arms encircle mother's neck while sucking thumb and preparing for slumber. A grade school teacher reads aloud to students who lean, hug, and suck on fingers against adult legs and feet. High fives and slaps to teammates in red and blue uniforms congratulate points and success. First kisses atop ferris wheels and against front doors occur with brushes of fingers intermingling with fingers. We need affection. Throughout life we seek physical affection, though the means to do so differentiates with age. We thrive from the affection of bodies pressed against each other in the fragrance of a hug, knowing both giver and receiver literally give and send cellular messages of comfort.

Athletes know chemistry and bonding of physical needs fulfilled. Sports develop commitment among individuals engaged in meeting physical needs with others. I led a line of orange and black pompoms to the rhythm of Fleetwood Mac and the dynamics of a winning team. I grasped the high peg of a climbing wall, while smiling upon a woman joined to me with ropes and rapelling equipment of support – inner and outer experiences of trust and letting go. My friend, Cathie, taught me to run. Okay, not putting one foot in front of the other … the whole rhythm of running and pacing breath. She patiently waited through my gasps, excuses, and sideaches. Cathie completed a five mile run for her birthday with smiling tears and a first place prize after we trained for two months. My husband grasped my shirt as I poured out against river pouring into our whitewater raft. We tumbled a high rapid and I rowed for survival. We won. Physical activity honors achievement and failure as bonded beyond words to others.

As a past theatre director and coach, I frequently hugged students to display my pride. Though my students are older, there are times of crisis when a hug is still needed: as brothers leave for Iraq; friends die; parents are diagnosed with illness. Laws prevent touch, to protect those who might otherwise be victims of power imbalances and unhealth. The laws are necessary and understandable, but touch is also a communicative extension of such understanding and affection: a necessary part of life. In fact, a touch on the shoulder of a distracted student, brings him/her back to fully present learning. Further, bodies are not sacred extensions of our being if we are using sexual affection to replace need for a hug. Physical needs are constant source of discernment and health.

Discernment allows us to live out our erotic selves openly, especially when women's enjoyment of sex is affected so greatly by psychological component. When we move into sexual relationship openly knowing emotional trust and reciprocation to our most intimate vulnerabilities, we experience the splendor of ecstatic *knowing* of pleasure fulfilled by another in complete wholeness, openness, and love. We are profoundly completed by another. Women who choose to engage in significant relationship are blessed in a union of ultimate trust and vulnerability as oneness of sexual pleasure expresses itself in loving nature, chemistry, and passion. *Communing* with whole self opened up to giving and receiving in unfathomable bliss.

Relationship Development: Necessary Conflict

We share information with others incrementally and we are amused by those who give us way too much information too quickly. For some reason, I seem to most often experience this discomfort while getting my hair done – when I'm "stuck" under a cape and cannot escape the details of the stylist's divorce, the "romantic interludes" of meeting complete stranger online ... complete with sexual details, and the list goes on. Normal levels of self-disclosure signify the health of the relationship because of the mutual reciprocation and the gradual development of intimate sharing. We are wise to question those who withhold information or don't respond in like. Further, we look to the person's actions as nonverbal extensions of the values they speak: do they walk the walk, or just talk the talk? The majority of our world is full of kind, loving people – but we all know the smooth-talkers, the charmers, who work their ways into our lives.

We all have experienced the pain of betrayal. We remember well the quills of porcupines who betrayed our trust. For me, I distinctly remember the awkward years of junior high and dating for the first time, amidst friends who betrayed me and told others of my crushes. It's no wonder we hesitate to share intimate, vulnerable information. However; holding onto pain of the past keeps us complacent rather than growing in relationship with others. We need to give and receive love. We need to trust – and reciprocate trust – especially after we've been hurt.

We develop the rituals that will allow us to let go of our deepest suffering, the ones who truly have "beat" us down. We refuse to remain "Beat". We ritualize a letting go, and we cognitively remember doing so in order to move on. We create a mantra through ritual and restructured cognition. We teach ourselves healing and put our hearts back out there. Our hearts and souls will catch up as well, in their own time. Rituals of healing bring us to our compassionate selves, without bitterness, remorse and regret. We view all relationships from a sacred space of contemplation. A new lens of paramount exquisiteness surrounds us and lavishes us with human relationships of compassion and love.

We look for consistency and commitment. Those who deceive cannot remain consistent. I once knew a man who e-mailed me in Spanish, only to tell me years later he didn't speak Spanish. So, I guess he actually unlearned Spanish. This red flag opened my eyes to other details that made no sense, and soon I discovered he was not about genuine caring. Reverent attentiveness to our relationships is mindful development maintenance for our inner spirit and health. Relationships end, and sometimes we exercise the choice to leave them.

Healthy relationships actually involve quite a bit of internal conflict: defining contours of Self and how we present our image to others. We are constantly balancing the need to be alone in order to achieve goals and voice ourselves with the need to be liked and affirmed by others. We actually need a balance of both. This is our clarity and health. Communicators call this *interdependence*. Transcendent experience of the same balance leads us to create who we are with divine in terms of how we may serve others with our gifts of love. We have a need to send loving energy and kindness to others: reaping and sowing and kharma. But we cannot do so if we are draining ourselves, rather than being fulfilled with what we need. Again, contemplative view allows us to name what we most need and move forward accordingly.

Healthy relationships are *interdependent*, rather than *codependent*. We don't depend on others without the power of depending on Self and development or growth of self. Co-dependent relationships don't respect individual growth for either party. Instead, they create fantasy of needing another for happiness, rather than happiness from within. Often, they become controlling. "I want to go, but I don't know if my boyfriend will **let me**." Submissiveness remarks may be signs of women involved in dysfunctional relationship. Relationships that need to terminate, yet continue to go on become dysfunctional and frustrating for both parties, who become each other's "crazymakers". Lovers become frustrated enemies. Two cars meet in an alley, and one must back up. Drivers emerge, hostile and screaming. A baby cries in an infant seat in back, red faces move into threatening proximity, policeman arrive. Many of us can relate to relationships that take us "out of ourselves" and into emotional places we don't want to relive – chaos instead of clarity. Fear instead of love.

"It's the quiet ones you have to watch out for," he whispered. My quietude was a result of my fidel relationship with my husband, yet he remained persistent when I explained. For me, it's the persistence that eventually turns a harmless line or compliment into, well, disgust. I called upon a healing mantra from years back. I know it comes as no surprise to you that some men and women are just looking for sex to gain intimacy, rather than intellectual and emotional bonding. It bears noting that stories in our culture define sex in relationships differently, therefore encouraging the problematic misunderstanding: males use it to achieve intimacy, while females use it to *culminate* feelings of emotional connectedness and intimacy. I've encountered a few men throughout my life who are looking for meaningless encounters, as have you if you're extroverted like I am. My mantra is a means to patiently wait out an exchange or closure of friendship from a place that maintains my wholeness and value, "I will always never have sex with you." That's it. That's what I do as self-talk to hold no anger or bitterness against the other as I move back into my self-worth and love. We continue to define ourselves only and especially in the purity of relationships that serve our goodness.

Co-dependent relationships are obvious to us with others because we are not emotionally engaged. Students lament lost friendships and roommates who no longer socialize with them, or when they do immerse in conversation by cellphone and text messaging with romantic other. Becoming addicted to people is destructive, hurtful, and even dangerous – as some relationships move into more controlling levels of abuse and/or even obsession. Sometimes people are living out motives of power and control and deception, rather than caring and compassion. Stop. Do not pass go. Do not collect $200. We needn't be monopolized, stopped or ignored by those who are not listening to our worth and the worth of our messages. We are not stuck, we are not paralyzed. We are holding the "get-out-of-jail-free" card the entire time in our spiritual knowing. Nobody has power over us, and feelings of fear are graces to lead women to clarity as they "see" the abuse or unhealth of their significant relationships. Our spirit moves us into our health and healing. We leave. We return to love and help others do likewise.

In the short story "Rocking Horse Winner" by D.H. Lawrence, a mother loves money more than her son. Sadly, Paul, the son lives and dies trying to please her misplaced desire for money and power. In life, others don't always recognize our value. Mindful discernment creates the lens to know who is worthy of our deepest affections, and who needs to be let go. Sadly, throughout life, relationships end. People are brought into our lives intentionally, but it's our obligation to listen to signs of closure and endings. Meanwhile, doors of opportunity open to meetings with other kindred souls when we pay attention. Helen Keller once remarked, "When one door of happiness closes, another opens; but often we look so long at the closed door that we do not see the one which has been opened for us."

Another source of conflict is inevitable: two people in relationships will experience differing needs. When we announce ourselves to the world, it may not like what it hears. We flee from conflict to avoid the pain. Conflict with another announces one of our greatest fears – that *the other might leave us*. The reason we don't voice our needs is always based in fear. We dare to name the fear and know when we are out of balance. Our greatest fear is that we will be left alone, isolated. Yet, our solitude of contemplative living teaches us we are never alone. All quality relationships fulfill a need we have, so the threat to losing that fulfilled need can be excrutiating. We deceive ourselves into believing the conflict will go away, fix itself. Instead, the frustration builds until there is all manner of shouting, anger, and emotional outburst. It's helpful to understand the nature of conflict as a necessary healthy component to intimate relationships.

It's easier to engage in ineffective behaviors of avoidance or procrastination rather than assertively discuss the facts of the problem, the feelings created, and an ideal solution. Focusing only on these areas avoids bringing in personal attacks and/or overemotional language. As we assert our wants/needs, we remember the other is often too busy to know these thoughts, or to even have time to be considering our place. We assume others know our feelings simply because we are feeling them. In fact, most often, others are wrapped up with their own feelings, issues and not even aware.

Asserting ourselves based on our needs and facts of being, takes the other off the defensive posture. So often, we mistakenly announce our needs by blaming which only serves to create distance. Naming our needs in terms of our caring about the other and the relationship illustrates our commitment to do the work of the relationship: resolution of conflict. So often, people leave when the going gets tough – we needn't remain in the pain of those who never really committed to us. Truthfully moving through conflict in open discussion conveys a new vulnerability and trust. Solving a problem together actually spirals the relationship into further intimacy and, if it's a significant other, some pretty amazing making up affection. We move from distance to understanding. Understanding allows us to view the world from the same lens.

We balance in solitude, naming own needs and needs in relationship with others in order to know when balance is off and we need to assert. Pronouncing and announcing. We need a sense of community, yet true inner growth is learning to love spending time in aloneness. Indeed, it is where we find our Selves. We are nourished differently each time we turn inward to pronounce ourselves more deeply, when we can also turn to intuitive self for emotional coping, comfort and growth. Sorting occurs in the fullness of silence and awareness. The clarity of pronouncing moves us to announce ourselves to others differently. True voice guides the nourishment of spirit in both cases. Sorting chaos and insanity of society is always constructive rather than destructive. Words of vulnerability are spoken, seen with rational perspective and dignity. Words sit in air and we view them differently from when they are screaming in our heads in desperation. Simply adding voice to chaotic thought brings clarity. Last evening, I had dinner with my husband and voiced internal chaos, named it. "I hope readers understand I face the same difficulties throughout life they do, otherwise I'm a hypocrite. I still get hurt, get betrayed, make mistakes. Only why do I feel a difference in the place I am now?" There. The words sat in air. But … the minute I gave voice to the frustration, it lifted. I saw the difference of growth.

I saw perspective and found my voice. Contemplative view of relationships *is* different: I surround myself with healthy relationships and sit with my sacred divine in contemplative experience. Embracing community with others names my pain and lets go of it. I'm holding onto no pain, though I've been hurt numerous times in life. I move through the pain in a healing manner and I continue to live life openly trusting others, though I've been betrayed. The spiritual lens provides transcendent understanding. Further, others who know me well embrace my pain and lovingly guide my healing with their compassion. We no longer are isolated in our pain, because we are communing with others as we move out of the pain and discover a letting go process. Further, we are created to live in this world with others – not as isolates. A gift of intimate sharing occurs only when we dare to trust and sort intimate issues. Sometimes we learn to let go of insult and injury, allowing a pink ball to carry those who hurt us far, far away. Sometimes we learn to laugh at ourselves in process. We let go of the stress of dissonant or conflict in relationships, rather than carry it in our physicality. We live in a state of healing and growth, rather than destruction and fear of isolation.

Conflicting Genders: Viva la Diference!

Clashing of these cultural views opens experiences of misunderstanding. Just as the understanding of other cultures eliminates unnecessary conflict and adds richness to our lives, so can we appreciate knowing about the stories of opposite gender. We benefit from understanding and living both perspectives, according to the needs of our wholeness. Indeed, we are all masculine and feminine with the beauty of choice to live according to discernment of needs as we move through life with connection and power, as women who lead.

Cultural differences between individuals can create a distance. We look toward understanding to bring us connectedness. Our culture tells stories of different gender expectations in communication. When we don't acknowledge these stories in order to live out of them in our unique manner, we cannot find our complete truth. When we are young, we learn to communicate with others very differently. Deborah Tannen, Ph.D describes masculine play as competitive, while feminine play is cooperative in her video *He Said, She Said Gender, Language & Communication* (2001). It's imperative to note that our culture's stories ritualize boys into a masculine communication style and girls into a feminine communication style, but they are truly gender styles which may include either sex. Further, we are wise to integrate and teach both styles to promote understanding between gender. Tannen gives the example of boys who are trying to outdo or "one-up" the other with building a tower. One boy states his can reach the sky, the other one says his can reach way to God. Clearly, the boy whose tower can reach way to God has "won". This is a very innocent type of game, and the boys know the other can't really build towers to the sky or to God, but it's all about the language of winning the competition. I would hear my sons talk to their friends in this manner, and want to interrupt, because I knew there was no truth in much of what was being said in the conversation. I now realize the game of their development. Additionally, the games of boys frequently include sports and include a large number of players. The rules are already established, so they play only for the goal of competition.

A classic study of children's play examines different rules of communication for each gender (Maltz and Borker, 1982). Boys' games cultivate three communication rules:

1. Use communication to assert yourself and your ideas; use talk to achieve something.
2. Use communication to attract and maintain an audience.
3. Use communication to compete with others for the "talk stage," so that they don't gain more attention than you; learn to wrest the focus from others and onto yourself.

These rules exist even into adulthood. The men in my classes frequently discuss videogames, frisbee golf, and drinking games as part of the continuation of this socialization. When they conflict with a close friend, they will physically fight it out or wrestle and then be friends again! It's all about the one-up or game of winning. A woman in significant relationship with a man may question why he doesn't engage in the vulnerability of relationship talk – or why he prefers to use sex (an activity) to initiate intimacy rather than as the culmination of emotional bonding of feminine perspective. Our culture creates different communication style for females.

Girls play very differently. A little girl screams, "a D-D-Dora Doll!" She hugs a felt figure larger than she and hugs and twirls and dances, and promises to sleep with her in her big girl bed. Our culture teaches feminine nurturing. Girls play with fewer numbers, many times with just one friend, and they cooperate with each other to form the play. My own experience included playing house, playing Barbie dolls, and playing make-believe concerts, school, or church. When I was about ten I was back-up singer for a band called "The DJ's" – representing the members: Debbie, Jeannie, and Julie. My friends and I sang a concert for the neighborhood complete with lemonade, cookies, and the back-up of a 45 record on a turntable playing Vicky Lawrence's "The Night the Lights went out in Georgia", and various hits by the Osmond brothers. We had to cooperate to decide who sang which song, what our attire would be, and who would choreograph the back-up. As little girls at play, we learned decision-making and learned to be considerate of the others' feelings. Indeed, cooperation becomes an integral part of the play for little girls.

Maltz and Borker identify three basic rules for communication in this play:

1. Use collaborative, cooperative talk to create and maintain relationships. The *process* of communication, not its content, is the heart of relationships.
2. Avoid criticizing, outdoing, or putting others down; if criticism is necessary, make it gentle; never exclude others.
3. Pay attention to others and to relationships; interpret and respond to others' feelings sensitively.

It follows women are better empathic listeners in adulthood – since that is the familiarity of their experience and culture. However, women who continue these rules into adulthood will find different expectations. A woman is weak when she uses only these rules in the workplace. Certainly, her voice will never be heard if she is not adapting to the masculine style of communication and sharing ideas assertively, bluntly, and even by interrupting to "one-up" and gain attention when needed. Conversely, a man is steroeotyped into believing his emotions are weakness and cannot be displayed. A man struggles to share relationship talk and a woman needs to emotionally connect with talk. Lack of understanding of cultural distances creates division rather than connection and conflict rather than resolution. Ultimate understanding is in respectful knowledge of both styles.

Relationships are tough stuff – especially when conflict arises and empathic listening seems distant. I saw a video that portrayed the way couples fought. According to this provocative research, the **way** in which a couple fights determines the success of the relationship. When the power of winning is played as a strategy it's easy to respond in kind. Soon, some couples fall into destructive behaviors of dredging up past issues and/or mistakes, namecalling, hurtful remarks and even mocking. Clearly, destructive behaviors such as these move both parties out of the work of respect and commitment and into a downward spiral of self in relationship with other. Need is not addressed or asserted as both move into egotistical need to one-up the other, rather than remember the commitment of connection.

We learn and teach the gifts of both perspectives. We pronounce and announce ourselves differently as masculine and feminine beings and come to stronger understanding and connectedness with others as a result of both. We are nourshed as we engage in both processes. His Holiness the Dalai Lama states:

> ***The more we focus on others, the more we have a concern for others, it seems to bring an inner strength.***

Daring to Rise: The Face-to-Face

Vending machines stand just outside my public speaking classroom. One day, soda cans were dropped just as a student began her speech. I spoke to the vendor and explained the situation. I respectfully asked if machines could be filled later, but they could not. He pondered. "I could just fill them quietly." And he did! I laugh every time I remember the simplicity of the resolved conflict because asserting a need face-to-face is such a valuable lesson. In fact, many conflicts are easily resolved with a simple, respectful conversation.

Spirits are always broken during conflict. Our bodies scream at potential loss of need the other fulfilled while spirits scream to return to wholeness. Further, if the other leaves, we may fear being alone. *External conflict is also conflict within. It's imperative we heal internal spirit and return to wholeness as we move into external healing in relationship.* College students tell stories of post-it notes and e-mailed breakups of those who couldn't or wouldn't do face-to-face and voice unexpressed need. Face-to-face is a mandatory first step in conflict resolution. We commit to the face-to-face with others and within.

Loneliness of isolation vs. Choice of Transformation

A woman prefers the company of cats to people ever since the man who loved her didn't love her cats. Like Miss Havisham in *Great Expectations* she was disappointed in love. She remained in polyester clothing and black, cat-like eyeliner of the seventies. She went home from work to her cats and exactly five drinks each evening. Socially isolated people are two to three times more likely to die prematurely than are those with strong social ties. The grade school child picked on by classmates for her highly hemmed pants and unkempt hair grows into an adult who continues to isolate.

Unless ... she becomes transformed in pain, rather than accepting of it. Face-to-face with inner child calls her to create the play and celebration of life through changed perspective. Research shows we need just one other, and silence allows us to *know* we deserve to live in interconnectedness with others. Buddhists are called to see goodness in others and view relationships from a state of kharma. Christians are called to serve as Christ and recognize those in pain, whose souls need wholeness. Happiness is birthed within. Says Picard, who wrote of silence in 1952:

> ***The substance of silence is necessary for re-creation, and it is also necessary for happiness. Happiness, which comes***

> ***down to man from the realm of mystery, is glad to find its way into the breadth of silence. There is immeasurability in happiness that only feels at home in the breadth of silence. Happiness and silence belong together just as do profit and noise.*** – Picard, *A World of Silence*

Pain and Loss.

A woman stands at the edge of the casket and fingers are raised unsure where to land as yearning for warmth of affection struggles against knowledge of coldness and death of physical self. Fingers hesitate and stroke lapels of a tweed suit jacket. Emblematic representations of kisses and hugs promised, but forever lacking. A body resonates coldness as mind and heart attempt to wrap meaning around experience. Numbness of thought cannot make sense.

We cling to relationships of intimate bonding and insist they remain, even when they've ended – literally or figuratively. Painful endings announce themselves to our hearts as sand sifting through fingers, though we are not yet ready to know pain. We grieve, we struggle, we are sliced in half as we question life experiences of loss. Bodies rise to innate nature to give love with no one to receive. We suffer in silence.

> ***Grief and silence also belong together. Grief achieves a poise in the breadth of silence. The force of the passions is lost, and grief, purged of passion, appears all the more clearly as pure grief. The lamentation in grief is transformed into the lamentation of silence. On the river of tears man travels back into silence.***
>
> – Picard, *A World of Silence*

We heal in solitude. We notice "something there" and know we are never alone. People are placed before us intentionally as parts of our deepest healing. We grieve as we open up to the angels guiding us back to wholeness. We gently hold integrity as our contemplative Self grows and reaches forth only, yet grandly, benevolently giving and receiving love, discovering growing edges and healing. Merton, a spiritual writer states, "We already have everything we need, we need only to remember." In the silence and solitude of our experience, we come to *know* this.

In the end, we remember the times we played with others; the times we slowed down and made memories and connection., and the times others made us feel wonderful. We received in those moments. What I miss most about the job I held for seventeen years is what we teachers knew of each other through play: a daily lunch game we played to determine who would carry the stack of lunch trays back to the dishwashers. We tallied points, and received pies and cakes at the end of each quarter to celebrate the "winner" with the most points. Students frequently remarked they could hear us laughing and shouting from the next room, the library. We used blowguns to pop balloons with messages, guessed trivia, engaged in competition of physical coordination, and even created our own rules for play. I look back on all meaningful relationships and savor the play and the beauty they held, not the pain of the endings.

I beheld a student in her greatness and talent a few years back. She phenomenally portrayed a character from a play entitled *Marks*. The character marked herself with a tattoo to represent or ritualize each person's effect or "mark" on her person. We are marked by others. Are the tattoos of love and laughter and happiness? Do we allow tattoos of constant hurt or destruction? Imagining the tattoos created by the wonder of people who come and go in our life gives vision of accepting only health and love. We are constantly in a state of healing or sickness amidst the people we interact with and we allow ourselves to view others in a reality created for us to become "something more". Indeed, we learn to appreciate the "someone more" of the person gently placed right before us and beside us.

> ***"Voices of the angels, ring around the moonlight***
> ***asking me, said she so free, how can you catch the sparrow?***
> ***Lacy, lilting lily, losing love lamenting, Change by life, make it right, be my lady."*** – Crosby, Stills and Nash

Chapter Six

Exquisite Love and Unfathomable Bliss

> ***This is an account of Satori, a spiritual enlightenment, a bursting open of the inner core of the spirit to reveal the inmost self. This takes place in the peace of what we might ordinarily call contemplation, but it breaks through suddenly and by surprise, beyond the level of quiet contemplative absorption, showing that mere interior peace does not suffice to bring us in contact with our deepest liberty.*** – Thomas Merton, *The Inner Experience: Notes on Contemplation*

Nothing is happening, yet fragments of everything are happening to senses. Time is frozen and timeless. *Communing* transcends communication and I commune with Christ as fingers slide on acoustic guitar in effortless bridge to Grace. *Amazing Grace.* I turn my head and butterfly wings in my heart turn me back to spirit. I notice. I notice my blind mother who now can see smiling on lyrics. I notice God beside me as others commune and I am vessel of spirit and wine. The spirit is an overflowing countenance to others lavishing forgiving love. The elderly woman in the leopard hat is kissing my cheek and blessing me. The young boy is looking up to me with somber brown eyes of hope and depth. The black woman humbles herself with eyes looking at the floor as she receives. The goblet is in my hand and I'm seeing God in all and I'm one with

God in the Amazing Grace of the moment. Beautiful connectedness. *Heartfelt knowing.* A new song begins as the soloist continues to sing the Amazing Grace over the dissonance of the new melody until the blend of harmony as lips kissing brings the consonance of joy. I pray. I am deeply touched. Words on a page on the same day, the same God time, explain the origin of lyrics to Amazing Grace. All is woven into the perfection of *bliss* and *knowing* … beyond rational experience is exquisite love, given and received. God *knows* me and I momentarily *know* God. The memory is carried with me and beheld in my chosen moments. All women deserve memories and the ultimate joy of *knowing*. Evocative, lavished love.

Definition of Personal Relationship: Lavished Love Awaits

We listen back and notice the Higher Good and soon move into a rhythm of being in conversation with the Higher Good. Just as we move through the stages of intimacy with human experience in relationship, so do we move into intimacy and trust in a personal relationship with Higher Good. When I let my intuition and sensual passion and heart move into spiritual experience, I am blessed with just what I need. In the way only God can create – with such perfect understanding and love. I spiral upward into deeper experience of love with God each time I am graced and am further motivated to use my passion to notice and listen. I reciprocate God's conversation. I give thanks I did and did not receive my life's prayers so my life's intricacy has formed this reality of love and compassion. I pray frequently now, opening myself to complete trust of the next step of my life journey. All individuals crave a personal knowing of God or the Higher Good. All human existence fades and is replaced with a soul magnificently touched in just the right moment, in just the right manner, according to individual need in divine relationship.

Our spiritual journey, which is lifelong, challenges us to grow in personal relationship with the Supreme Being. We name our concerns, sort them, and resolve to move into life experience with countenance and growth and openness. All faiths find freedom in spiritual understanding and growth and in working toward joy and the "something more" that is the richness of our human experience. Our human relationships meet the various parts of our selves, yet personal relationship with the Higher Good meets the whole Self and graces all women with responses to needs in just the right manner, I cannot help but burst forth toward others with the joy of the *knowing*. Journeying with our Selves creates an experience of unique love transcending any we have ever known. Our mothers provide us with unconditional love, our fathers provide us with the courage to move into life, lovers bring connection with our souls, and the Mother/Father God gifts us with all – beyond what we can possibly imagine. The knowing of our personal relationship brings us an internal joy to carry us through our human experience. Knowing acceptance and forgiveness gives us an inner strength of peace and understanding and connection we can take out to others in all of our most valued relationships. We are forever transformed.

The light of personal relationship with others brings us pleasure that is external and fades. The fire of personal relationship with transcendent relationship brings us a joy and knowing that is lavished upon our internal self and oozes into creation. The benefits of such include a countenance perceived as something attractive to others and a remarkable connectedness to all souls, allowing us to lead others to same power. Once we experience, we cannot go back – we refuse the emptiness of our previous gray experience.

In my humbleness I've accepted my weaknesses and horrible, horrible parts of myself because when I put these very parts out there for God to see, I receive only love, acceptance, and forgiveness when I listen back.

Because my own Christian image of God accepts me, I accept me. I grow in confidence and strength and the acceptance is a stronger, truer form of power than I've ever known. It's *divine power*. A student describes an aesthetic moment of grace in her divine power. She is learning to play guitar and is too unsure to yet play for others. She plays for her image of God and lyrics are created amidst chords that are no longer right nor wrong. *All is Right.* The musical experience takes her deeper. She is communing with God. She moves from a bad day experience – naming a healing vision of disappointment and aloneness lurking underneath. She feels. She notices. She sorts and she sings. She receives only love in a cascade of warmth spreading through her and resonating in her fingertips, touches of nylon harmony. There is no discord. She *knows* her deepest truth in this moment where all is right and all is okay and all is love. She yearns to play, to continue to deepen an intimate, personal relationship. Unlike the pain of our most loving human relationships sometimes ending in a brief whisper, God doesn't leave. She is no longer alone. She is loved. It's all love.

Removing Barriers

The lens of my current reality brings me to the most difficult barrier I placed in front of me in becoming intimate in relationship with God. Wondering how God could possibly want me, use me as a vessel for anything – held me back and restricted me. Once I faced that it was "even" me, I moved into *knowing. We* all hold ourselves back. *We* place the barriers. *We* are afraid and build the gray, cold dividing blocks of conflict and distance. *We* are afraid to feel our own holiness. For so long, I created a barrier of self-deception. I would have to be perfect if I chose my spiritual path. I would need to do more and more in order to be "good enough" – and that frightened me. As my journey opened up, I let go of my excuses and, in time (mine and God's), I knew my *just being* with giving and receiving love was splendidly enough. I stopped deceiving Self.

We distance from our Selves by numbing our senses and therefore, creating an aversion to noticing. Addictions to external desires, unnecessary medications, and misplaced desire are dividing our souls and fogging our conscience into believing we live the limits of our perceived reality. Personal relationship with God shows us the simplicity of *knowing* grander pleasure and limitless potential. Growth allows us to become absolutely limitless in fulfilling our joys and place in the world.

We continue to place barriers of punishment. We deceive ourselves with believing we need to beat ourselves up with shame, guilt, and abuse in order to be "good enough". What if the perceived reality is erroneous and we are already "good enough"? Indeed we are. We move out of addictive needs and into enjoying sensual beauty and attempt to do Right without the desire for perfection – which only cycles into further feelings of shame, guilt, and abuse. Supreme Being celebrates with our human experience of pleasure. The Higher Good wishes us joy and pleasure. I'm firmly convinced my God is right there with me as I savor the pleasures of a rich pasta dish, a moment in the sun, the texture and color of a fabric, an incredible experience of making love, and even the smooth cold/hot burn of a very good martini. Being about intimate relationship with God does not mean we deprive ourselves of earthly pleasure. In fact, we celebrate pleasure in a newfound way removed of our dependency for it. The very foci of our pleasure can be inward experiences of sensual joy rather than external attempts of satisfaction. The mystical occurrences which become our very memories and images of transformation allow us to see as Julian of Norwich did:

> ***I know well that heaven and earth and all creation are great, generous and beautiful and good. ... God's goodness fills all his creatures and all his blessed works full, and endlessly overflows in them. ... God is everything which is good, as I see it, and the goodness which everything has is God.***

Our images of Supreme Being come with such clarity of vision meeting our multiple layers of need for mother/father/creator/comforter/friend/lover and we move into a Supreme Being who only desires blessings and love. The reality of our perceptions is skewed by Western thought. Perhaps the most significant book to initiate the passion of my own spiritual journey is *Original Blessing* by Matthew Fox. I found such relief in his words about a creation-based God. He so beautifully connects all religions in a spiritual focus.

Spirituality connects while religions can potentially divide. The choice of religion is respectfully individual and cannot be "wrong" as long as it moves the individual closer to a greater Good, Love, and Acceptance. We overcome the very barriers of our current existence as presented by some religious establishments. I'm presently working with women who need to heal the shame and guilt of Pre-Vatican II teachings. Shame and guilt can easily create distance or avoidance from the very grandest love we seek – that of a Supreme Being. The overuse of horrible images of fear and damnation only serve to make us feel the more negative affect of guilt and shame and spiral us further downward. We dare not speak to a God who judges for fear of condemnation and may even avoid such a God. In our experience of moving out of the perceived realities in our heads into the simplicity of our hearts that know desire for and from God, we experience the grandest freedom of knowing we are accepted and loved, even in our sin. My individual desire to do right comes from a loving place of wanting to reciprocate my God's love rather than a fearful place of "making sure" I get to heaven. If you gain nothing else from my words, know this: God is only love for you and waiting to grace you with gifts beyond what can be fathomed – even with your weakness, even with your sin. It is our very weakness and humility that are transforming us into the blessing of our strength and empowerment. We need only name our needs and ask. Mathew Fox says:

> ***The prophets and others who disturbed the status quo did not seek only justice. They sought blessing, blessing for the many, not just for the few. It paid and paid well and is still paying well (witness, for example, the financial success of fundamentalist preachers on television) to keep guilt going and self-doubt going and distrust going, all in the name of an avenging God. To drown out the God of blessing is a powerful political act. But such silencing cannot go on forever. The God of Dabhar and of blessing does not tolerate being dammed up for long. She has too much Eros, too much love of life, too much desire to share the blessing and delight in our response to it. God's ecstasy will not forever be forgotten. Is that what Jesus the Christ came to remind us about?*** – Matthew Fox, *Original Blessing*

It's all love. It's all relief and simplicity of *knowing* love and taking it out to others. Respect and value become natural by-products of our new reality of walking through our human experience. Love is granted according to our most intimate desires and needs, and we share our love in presence with others.

Once we experience the mystical, we cannot quiet ourselves. We are busting out with the joy and laughter we experienced as children. We savor and enjoy the opportunities of this life and move into Authenticity and Truth in communication with others. As my trendy clothing, pierced belly-button, and love of rock'n'roll so clearly illustrate the product of pop-culture that I am, I also embrace the precious *knowing* of my unique gift and place in the world I am *becoming*. My relationships become deeper connections. True connections. Even *holy* connections.

Welcoming Our God

Just as we prepare for our guests and special relationship with fine wines, hors d'oeuvres, and delightful cuisine, we welcome or host our Supreme Being in our moments in silence. We set aside distractions and make ourselves comfortable. We remove ourselves from the limits of time, knowing God's time is never our own and is timeless in its grace. We quiet our thoughts and set them aside as we prepare to breathe into our calm, peace, holiness. We learn to quiet our mouths after speaking our prayers and flow into the meditation of our listening and noticing. We find a space that is safe from the interruptions of our busyness. We ready ourselves, we quiet our Selves and our thoughts, and *we know* we are in sacred, precious territory. Phillip Sheldrake speaks of this place:

> ***Place also has the capacity to reveal and evoke the sacred or the deepest meaning of existence. This transcends what can be uttered or ultimately known. It has a transformative effect because at that moment and in that place our inmost selves stand exposed and naked. Sacred place or, better, the sacred quality of place, is where the timeless and the deep can be found and in this is both grace and revelation.*** – Phillip Sheldrake, *Spirituality and Theology: Christian Living and the Doctrine of God*

Stillness allows us to evoke our needs and passions, discern our life choices, and experience heartfelt direction. Religions of all cultures regard this place as holy and nurturing.

The strength we experience in our truth is taken back out to the lens with which we view and honor our relationships. For example, I'm writing in strength/hope of forming an individual relationship with you. I'm led by pieces of my reality brought to me in just the right time and in just the right way to birth a book of connectedness, vision, and inspiration. The fact you are still reading affirms a mutual attraction and desire for what William James referred to as *something there* that guides us to *know something more.* The fact you can let go and move into the style of my "stream of consciousness" writing means you have opened up to possibility with my virtual reality – my perceived reality of hope, feminine connection and power. In a serendipitous moment during my writing, I discovered William James as creator of this writing style – a noticing of something more which affirms my own passion that you are, indeed, *someone more.* Further, you are *someone* of connection who is open to valuing Self in Kohlberg's post-conventional rather than conventional stage. You dare to question, to allow for possibility, to move into the higher good of your Self-awareness. I image my God smiling upon me as I write the words that become pages. I intuit the phenomenal experience of knowing I am not capable of writing this book alone. I image your God or Divine smiling upon you as you receive my message according to your own manner and understanding. I image your Divine helping you write the book of your life. Our Gods situate themselves arm-in-arm, smiling, and asking us to open up and become. Our Gods image the personal relationship of our experiences truly lighting the lights that connect as in a city as all women become. Let it magnificently *be* …

Discernment

As we host the Supreme Being in the here and now, we sort. Our life experiences bring us various decisions to make and some are small and some seem to blindside us unexpectedly. It seems our time is never congruent with the timing life gives us to make changes. So many of us still hold on to our safe places out of fear and make no changes. We truly need a base and support for a rationally thought-out human experience, but we are missing so much more by not being present to the moment. Contemplative silence and interpersonal relationship with Supreme Being bring us the richness of seeing life in the moment, sensually savoring the "something more" of our worldly experience. The lens of our truth guides the decisions of our life experience, just as Henri Nouwen wrote more than sixty years ago:

> ***Should I go to school or look for a job, should I become a doctor or a lawyer, should I marry or remain single, should I leave my position or stay where I am, should I go into the military or refuse to go to war, should I obey my superior or follow my own inclination, should I live a poor life or gain more money for the costly education of children?*** – Henri Nouwen, *Reaching Out*

We learn to stay with our present experience and listen to spiritual direction. We cannot feel the divine in the past, we cannot feel Higher Good in the future. We are blissfully forced to stay with the experience. We engage in heartfelt presence rather than cognitive analysis that leads us to presuppose anything we want about past and future and may not be our truth. We move out of our heads and into our hearts to discern our life journey and return to our heads knowing with such clarity what choice to make. I suffered dreadfully as I discerned which steps to take in my vocation. About a year ago I realized, through contemplation, that there are no wrong answers, it's about the process and the richness of growing into our authority. Like enjoying my morning run and trying not to "get there", I've learned the patience of knowing it can't be wrong, it's the beauty of the journey. It's not the *what* I do with my life, it's the *how* I do with my life in terms of giving and receiving love … the rest is detail. There's such a relationship with God/Supreme Being to sort life decisions, knowing God/Supreme Being always takes the initiative in coming to us, if we are listening and noticing. We will always struggle with moments of shame or guilt or anger when we are distanced from Higher Good but as we grow in relationship, we know we come to

Higher Good even, and especially, in times of shame and guilt and anger. In the end, it's transcendentally communicative – we have the freedom to choose whether to respond, ignore, or accept His/Her voice that is always focused toward deeper right or goodness.

Graces

My own experience is one of complete joy. I wake up in the morning with energy. I look forward to each day with the opportunity of what it brings. I wish I could say I no longer suffer, or that I no longer have bad days, but there will always be suffering. In the midst of even the most painful moment, my lens becomes one of hope and compassion. I am surprised with countless blessings of what I need – I listen and notice. I am given just what I need in the way it is needed to continue on my spiritual and human path as I walk the intersection of spiritual and human experience. Sufferings frequently bring loneliness. Indeed, I suffer from loneliness but am graced with a different attitude toward being alone. Karl Rahner, a German Jesuit theologian consulted for his expertise during the Second Vatican, eloquently refers to this perception change as "a terrible loneliness transformed into a rich solitude." In personal relationship with the Higher Good we learn to love the alone rather than dreading it. Ironically, we move into *knowing* we are never alone. *We choose to be with our holiest connection.* We receive Grace.

All humans desire knowing the "something more" of a personal relationship of connectedness. For me, it was the sight of a man praying in the solitude of a church. He stood with hands folded on top of a piano, directly in the ray of sun pouring down from the window above and shining in his blonde strands of hair. I remember the cream turtleneck of his posture showing such involvement and intense passion and it moved me deeply. I was visualizing folded hands and grandest connection. I immediately knew I wanted what he was experiencing. Walking in on such an intimate moment stirred me--I knew I wanted *something more.* I wanted the trust, openness, and passion exemplified by the snapshot of this moment.

We are surrounded by the yearning for intimate relationship with the Spirit. Our yearning is the vision to embark on life's quest for bliss and to fight the inertia of remaining in our "safe", familiar places with limits and guardedness. Our hearts yearn to do good. We don't turn back because we know the empty existence of the before. We intuit the emotions of others in need of love as we view their negativity: restlessness, crabbiness, and complaining, through the lens of our *knowing* and *love.* As vessels of spiritual truth, we guide others away from the energy suckers of our earthly experiences. Our countenance shows movement from temporary fixes in Ego toward fullness of Eros. Eros brings focused passion, wholeness, completeness. We give energy to others and are lavished by the Holy Spirit of "something more" to energize us toward further acts of compassion and love. We are moved to empowerment and justice and act accordingly. Just as the gentlemen who were aboard the flight on 9/11 which was directed toward the White House may have been guided. In their final moments they chose to fight for good instead of evil. Perhaps their intuitive spirit guided courage. They are heros. We too, are capable of heroic action when we know our truest strength. God guides us to accomplish the inconceivable. With God, *all is possible.* Dare to live your *all.*

Amazing Grace and Divine Purpose

Scripture proclaims that this love, from which and for which we are created, is perfect. I do not presume to fully understand what this perfect love means, but I am certain that it draws us toward itself by means of our own deepest desires. I am also certain that this love wants us to have free will. We are intended to make free choices.

> ***Psychologically, we are not completely determined by our conditioning; we are not puppets of automatons. Spiritually, our freedom allows us to choose as we wish for or against God, life, and love. The love that creates us may be haunting, but it is not enslaving; it is eternally present, yet endlessly open.*** – Isaiah 43:4 and 54:7-10

Freewill allows us to act from a place of love and also to **choose** love. We discern our human experience according to the needs of our true souls. And we have complete freedom from boundaries of fear and confusion. In our spiritual experience we choose from our hearts knowing God's love is unconditional. We search to emulate a relationship of interdependence with another. The divine understanding allows us to grow in our manner without restrictions and restraints of force. We *choose* God because we desire to in our Eros, not because we have to. And the divine *always* chooses us. We are left with the desire to know our true place in this world, our power in this world, our authority in this world.

Through the awkwardness of adjusting to silence with our being and with Being, we come to a mindfulness and reflective place which **leads** us to more, indeed, which **calls** us to more. Indeed, we are all called to realize and live our **holiness** and divinity walking through human experience as spiritual beings. We are led to our truth and we are liberated along the path. We empty ourselves of our addictions, our fears, our issues with life and others, and we fill ourselves with a met desire to know more, to be more, to "get there". Simultaneously, we walk in knowing we will never "get there" but we will forever be abundant with joyful moments in the path of human experience.

It's not the journey, it's the awareness of truth in journey through a growing, deepening, transforming, communing relationship with "something more." We stop abusing ourselves and begin *dis*abusing ourselves and moving into only Love. What was ordinary becomes Extra-ordinary.

We stop measuring our lives by our relationships with others and our material and intellectual successes. We move into the value of our spiritual lens of love toward others. Grow and live your Amazing Grace. Welcome Spiritual Relationship.

> ***Of course, the spiritual part of our lives is usually the first to be squeezed out by day to day pressures. St. Francis de Sales said we need half an hour every day for prayer and spiritual reflection – except when we are really busy and under pressure. Then we need at least an hour.***
>
> -- David Alton, a writer from *Universe Column* (June 30, 2002)

> ***Tis grace that brought me safe thus far, and grace will lead me home.***
> ***When we've been there ten thousand years, bright shining as the sun,***
> ***We've no less days to sing God's praise, than when we first begun.***
>
> – John Newton

Chapter Seven

Welcoming Spirit: A Variety of Religious Experiences

What is vast emptiness? It is sunyata – the womb. The source. It is the source of all things. It is not empty in the sense we are used to, but full of potential, full of energy.
– *The Unknown She*

A contemplative presence refers to a reverent attentiveness to the spiritual director's experiences and God's presence. An atmosphere is created in which such attentiveness can take place. An evocative approach. – *Looking into the Well*

The warmth of the leather of the chair and the steam of my morning coffee comfort me as I softly waken to splendid indigos, pinks, and orange yellows in the azure contour of a morning sunrise. I sit and I am silent. I am listening without listening and noticing without noticing. My thoughts are as clouds floating in and out of consciousness and perception. I enjoy. I calm. Cool air refreshes the tip of my nose with positive energy and I exhale the warmth of negativity, cleansing my body and soul. In my meditation, I awaken to sensual awareness creating the nuance of a created day. I am fully present.

It is later and I am praying while making my lunch. I hold the potato given to me in love because it is organic and raised only with purest care, nurturing, and love. The love transforms into shreds moving through the antique gratings of my mother's kitchen device. I watch as I push to change shape and form of organic love into sustenance and satisfaction. I marvel in the simplicity, purity, and care given by each of the pieces to my cooking and I know my body is blessed. I pray as I work knowing the energy of love in the making is healing to my physical form and I savor the potato that becomes so much more in the making. In my meditation and in my prayer, I am mindful.

Our varieties of spiritual experiences are numerous, varied, and intricately individual, yet all are mindful. It matters not **how** we meditate or pray, only **that** we meditate and pray – for our Selves, our Healing, and our Welcoming of Spiritual Relationship. As we grow, we listen and notice. We incorporate new images of Supreme Being and new ways to welcome oneness and conversation. Meditation is silent in its connectedness. Prayer is silent and/or active. We choose according to the needs of our Truth and our path. And we are never wrong. Our desire alone to meditate and pray and connect with "something more" is also a prayer that is individually holy. To be mindful is to be fully present and welcoming to spiritual personal relationship. Meditative focus is oneness, prayerful focus is transcendent dual relationship.

Continuing a spiritual path begins with individual choice to accept and/or reject belief systems and/or religions based on individual need and reverence, according to individual contemplative discernment. As such, mindful reflection and/or prayer are to be respected and revered. In the end, there is only one true Supreme Being manifested to many cultures with many mystical stories and word forms. *Communing* with spiritual body within the Self leads to *commun*ity with others toward service and justice in just the right manner for individual spiritual path.

Meditative Mindfulness

We are just getting started. Listening to inner truth allows us to touch so many. Thich Nhat Hanh is a Vietnamese Buddhist monk and author of *The Miracle of Mindfulness* (1999). He intensely worked for peace during the Vietnam War. He is over seventy years old and is still banned from Vietnam for work he did when he was forty. He worked ceaselessly to connect or reconcile North and South Vietnam with calm and peace from within. Though he was ironically banned as "threat" for his work toward peace, he continued to teach and to show many about peace through meditation, and spirit of awareness of Self, others, and justice. A very general search of Thich Nhat Hanh's work shows he taught mindful awareness on college campuses in the United States and to many college administrators, political figures, and social dignitaries. I admire his ability to draw a diverse audience connected only in mindful spirit, connected only in being present and aware:

> ***For at least a decade, Thich Nhat Hanh has visited the United States every other year; he draws more and more people with each tour, Christian, Jewish, atheist, and Zen Buddhist alike. His philosophy is not limited to preexistent religious structures, but speaks to the individual's desire for wholeness and inner calm. In 1993, he drew a crowd of some 1,200 people at the National Cathedral in Washington DC, led a retreat of 500 people in upstate New York, and assembled 300 people in West Virginia. His popularity in the United States inspired the Mayor of Berkeley, California, to name a day in his honor and the Mayor of New York city declared a Day of Reconciliation during his 1993 visit.***
>
> – Thich Nhat Hanh as cited on http://www.seaox.com/thich.html

Additionally, Dr. Martin Luther King, Jr. nominated Thich Nhat Hanh for the Nobel Peace Prize. Dr. Martin Luther King Jr. so bravely led many in nonviolent protest during the civil rights movement. The spirit of one human has reached so many. Imagine the world as we all move into our growing edges, our challenges to become limitless in intent toward peace and good. We limit when we believe only ego has power. Power of spirit is limitless. Remarkably, we believe change can only come from a group, yet it always begins with one spirit. Beginning is awareness and spiritual path is power. We are called to find spirit and listen to intuition. Supreme Being gives all we need in just the right way, in just the right manner. We need only notice the graces and live in gratitude and trust.

Another man to deeply affect so many is the Dalai Lama. The Dalai Lama teaches us to mindfully consider the practice of "Achieving Calm Abiding":

1. An *initial cause*, morality, brings a peaceful, relaxed, conscientious mode of behavior and thus removes coarse distractions. This stage is called placement.
2. A *time and place* for practice apart from the commotion of daily life. Make time for mediation in your daily schedule. For focused meditation, being alone in a secluded, quiet spot is crucial. Since noise is the thorn preventing concentration, at the beginning it is very important to stay in a quiet place. Consider taking a retreat for your vacation.
3. A suitable *diet* fostering clarity of mind. For some health conditions, it may be necessary to eat meat, but, generally speaking, vegetarian food is best. Also eating too much food is not good, so eat less. Of course, drinking alcohol is out of the question, as are all mind-altering drugs.
4. The right amount of *sleep*. Too much makes your mind dull, and too little can be disruptive. You have to figure out what the right amount is for you.

5. Physical posture is critical to focused meditation.

The first researched proof of healing through meditation was only recently reported. A year ago, I read about an experiment done near the University of Madison (Wisconsin) with a neuroscientist, Dr. Richard Davidson and a well-known meditation guru, Jon Zabat Zinn. Employees in a company engaged in meditation and/or prayer for a six-week period on a daily basis. The result was a literal change in cognition toward what they termed "happiness set point". In terms of my meager understanding of brain, I suggest that right brain experience of spiritual calm later transfers over to left brain rational message of "okayness" that changes lens of view of both daily and life experience. Interestingly, two months later, they found a long-term result of constant heightened "happiness set point". It's amazing to see proof of what we already *know* in our *being*. Truly, we affect our Selves, our lives, our spiritual being in every interpretation of thought on cellular and spiritual level. We heal when we strengthen our cognition of "okayness" – and every moment we are healing or destroying.

Meditation brings Oneness and acceptance. Physical posture removes dissonance and moves into assonance and harmony of *communing with* in all of our physicality. Yoga is a divine opening up of physical being. Each chakra opens through the series of movements in such a manner to bring absolute bliss. I visualize the "survival" chakra we often remain in, which is located just near the solar plexis. I know this from my public speaking students who often place their hand subconsciously over this same area when up in front and experiencing fear. Need to feel safe prevents us moving up into head, the chakra where all beings can spend time in spirit. Yoga allows me to visualize the literal and figurative openings of chakras as healing energy climbs upward along the spine, throat, and into the top of the head bursting with pink light into the wellness and wholeness of complete energy. I let go of need for safety and fear when I discern in meditation and prayer, and allow spirits to fully be up in my head with Supreme Being. Through yoga, I rest in the warmth of knowing I've "gotten there" temporarily as the session cools down, and bliss wraps me gently.

Prayerful Mindfulness

Prayer can extend or replace the meditative experience for those who choose to move into active personal relationship with Supreme Being. The quietude of prayer can bring divine love for solitude. Prayer can also be active, and I am an active person. I pray while running, while driving (!), while dancing, and while walking my dog. I talk, I sort, I listen, and I move into resolution, comfort, and peace.

Prayer is calming. Prayer of soothing words while I nestle in a deeply concaved leather-seated rocking chair of an ancestor's spirit brings womblike comfort. Rote prayer of rosaries and evening and dinnertime prayers allow possibility of wandering into heart and noticing of divine response. Nightime tucking and prayer move children out of need for safety and into opportunity to know divine love. Chanting and repetition invite heartfelt movement and mindful familiarity of divine.

Posturing creates various tones or moods toward gratitude, suffering, and reconciliation. Praying while lying on my bed snuggled in pillows and blankets resonates a warmth of comfort. Praying while kneeling expresses submissive reality of a woman in need or a time of gentle humility. Prayers of gratitude are wide open spaces and my body embraces as I lay in the lush, green blades of grass, or the heat of the sandy beach beneath. Supreme Being grandly connects with us in purest, Truest form. Deer roaming in woods in search of food in the melting snow, breathing in the fresh cool of a winter snow and capturing moments of bright blue serenity amidst gray/white swirls of a growing, cleansing rain become prayers because they are connectedness to nature--all created by divine. All are graces when we open up to *communing* with world and *communion* with God.

Journaling prayer allows me to look back and see answered prayer. Additionally, it allows me to see prayers that weren't answered affirmatively, and likely, shouldn't have been. A journal allows a glimpse of the bigger picture of relationship. My journal presents the path of grand plan and spiritual growth. The most difficult times of prayer and suffering were the teachable moments of my life – and I'm grateful for even them. Prayers of gratitude multiply with our listening and noticing. Variety of prayer allows for variety of blessings and ecstatic response. All combine to create an intricately woven spiritual path, the threads of which are rich and meaningful. Walking from one spiritual noticing to another creates a spiritual path of growth and change. Just as my students discern values instilled by parents, so do we discern owning our own spirit and center.

My favorite prayer is ongoing opportunity to come back to scripture or base. Roots of spirit and religion are pure and authentic. My Christian experience of reading the Bible filled me with an experience of *knowing* Trinity in it's inception. I want others to fully experience bliss in this manner. *Lectio Divina* (Holy Reading) is a reverent manner of praying with scripture. My soul is repeatedly transformed in the beauty of this experience as guided by the Benedictine Sisters:

1. Quiet the body and mind and pray for the Spirit to lead you.
2. Read slowly once or twice, Sacred Scripture, a reading, or reflect on a life experience.
3. Meditate, go deeper, reflecting on that word or phrase, imagine the scene, think of what it means to you. Make connections with your life.
4. Prayer. Speak to God about your experience. Listen to what God says to you. Become aware of the presence of God.

5. Contemplate. Rest in that reflection, insight, prayer or feeling. Rest in the presence of God.
6. Compassion. We share this experience of God and send out a prayer of love to a person(s). You may decide to do a specific action for someone.

Close with a prayer of gratitude.

I also engage in *Lectio Divina* with music lyrics, knowing the instrumentals of music can greatly enhance a necessary mood for deepening thought into heart and mystic experience. Music moves heart into prayer. Poetry read in this manner leads to experiencing rhythm of words and rhythm of life.

Mindfulness and Vocation

I'm enthused to see so many bring individual authentic knowing into daily experience of work. Further, we are all called to find our gifts in vocation, and be lead into the energy and joy of serving. Prayer space is sacred and necessary at home and at workplace. I keep seven river stones on my office desk to hold as I meditate and pray. A coworker breathed words of knowing as he passed by. He knows meditative energy and our spirits briefly connected. We talked of removing walls and doors and connecting all spirits into healing for truest potential.

I attended a Faith Conference in Minneapolis attended by clergy and business people. I was awestruck to hear speakers from Fortune 500 companies share intimate conversation of creating prayer spaces in offices. One leader moves into a small prayer room to discern all decisions for his major finance company. Another leader speaks honestly of her personal desire to have relationship with her God. I'm touched as we speak briefly after the presentation, and her creamy, silk blouse reminds me of the stunning and polished attire necessary for someone in her position. I will perhaps never wear a blouse with such exquisite texture and yet, we are conversing openly and honestly and connecting about spirit. Immeasurable connection contrasting a human experience measured with richness of textured brand-name clothing, pearls, and elegance. I see deeply into the soul of a woman of such stature as she smiles and we are *communing*. In the end, **she** asks **me** for a business card. All is possible. We share *breath*, or *espiritu*.

Interestingly, quite a few Americans actually engage in prayer/ inner spirit to make decisions in corporate world. A book from the State of Faith Conference in Minneapolis confirms what is truth for leaders in our country:

> ***A recent poll reveals that when one looks beyond Wall Street, U.S. executives as a whole tend to be at least as ethical, religious and spiritual as the average American adult. In some cases they are even more devout in their religious beliefs and expressions. The results come from a survey conducted between May 13 and June 6, 2002, by our firm, Lawrence Research of Santa Ana, Calif. We interviewed a random national sample of 500 business executives, defined as company owners, officers, executives, directors, or managers.***

The results spoke volumes. The survey revealed 82% talked decisions over with colleagues – which is not surprising. However, 74% prayed for help or inspiration! While I'm curious how "prayer" was defined, I applaud the results. Although it is rightfully illegal to enforce or persuade others toward religious choice, it is rightfully legal to embrace deepest spirit with power and connection. When we embrace all essence of Supreme Being in others, we can look to our leaders with respect and reverence. Individual meditation and prayer affirm decisions toward mission through ownership and highest ethical values. Spirits of coworkers laugh and play, removed from the ego of conflict. Spirituality is interconnectedness when all breathe together. Religious choice or preference as persuasion divides – and it should. Individual choice is the richness of a spiritual journey as it's intended.

My current spiritual path is leading me to a class in mediation (conflict resolution in the workplace). Indeed, wholeness is resolved conflict: intrapersonally, interpersonally, and on larger scale. I'm delighted to see professionals embracing spiritual lens among conflict resolution in the workplace. I'm reading a series of articles in *ACResolution* which is the quarterly magazine of the Association for Conflict Resolution. An article by Daniel Bowling speaks of using mindfulness in the process of mediation. His work is quite related to our journey of contemplative listening. Bowling traces the origin of the word "present" to the Latin *(pre) praesens, praesent*, meaning "to be before: in the sense of to be before one at hand." He continues:

> ***Thus, presence is being exactly where we are and mentally where we are and mentally focused before whoever is with us in this moment of now. Presence is possible only when we are aware now, not lost in the past or future. Presence expands as we elevate our own healing and is therefore developmental, not magical. Presence is the context for resolving conflict.*** – Daniel Bowling, *Who Am I as a Mediator? Mindfulness, Reflection and Presence* (Fall, 2005)

Indeed, mindfulness, contemplative listening, and presence are concepts embraced by national professions in mediation and litigation. Success in workplace notices importance of being fully present to employees for success in conflict resolution, respect for employees and clients, and mission. Return on investment occurs as organic byproduct of pure intent in vocation. We remember to move out of complacency and into action of becoming transcendent in view. Kenneth Cloke, J.D., Ph.D., L.L.M., who is the Director of the Center for Dispute Resolution in Santa Monica, California states:

> ***Conflict is simply a place where people are stuck and unable to be relaxed or authentic, and by learning to become unstuck, they can discover how to transcend not only that conflict, but also similar conflicts.***

We are not stuck, though ego leads us to fear and paralysis. Contemplative lens leads to clarity and focused passion of action. Clearly, Cloke echoes the growthful process of identifying inner truth and authenticity through transcendent discernment of self or contemplative listening.

Family law also includes a recent paradigm reflecting a need for contemplative listening. In an article titled "The Spiritual Aspects of Collaborative Law" by Dale Raugust, the following advice is given to family law attorneys:

> ***You can enjoy competing, and have fun in a world where winning is regarded as "fun", but "winning" in family law is inappropriate. It is not about winning. It is about responding to people who are expressing fear based emotions with compassion and understanding; listening to them and really understanding their emotions; then creating an environment in which they are made to feel respected and understood so that they can start the process of healing. Let go of your need to win. That is your ego's fear. When you give up your need to win, you also give up your need to be right. Ego pushes you in the direction of making other people wrong.***

Life is not about right and wrong – life is about what is true. I fully intended to point out the need for businesses and workplaces to embrace wholistic healing of contemplative listening to bring authenticity to others and mission. I'm so pleasantly surprised to see so many who already know. It's imperative in our world. Vocations not tied to calling and authenticity drain us and hold back the sacred responsibility of serving others. Living a calling rediscovers deepest joy and playful living. Life becomes fun.

Rediscovering Joy of Childhood

It's remarkable how close to Supreme Being children's experience can be – and I wonder why our culture teaches priority of rational until we can no longer remember the purity of our intimate existence and the organic process of joy and laughter, without fear of safety. Ask children what their Divine looks like and they can tell you. Ask children what Divine says to them and they know. I heard a child remark with such enthusiasm, "Come on! Let's go outside and see what God has made us!" Do we notice beauty and divine presence in nature? Remembering innocence and divine power leads to an awakening of child images. One college student sees connectedness of energy in the universe through her junior high best friend as image. Another student sees a veil of smoke that colors according to mood and circumstance. One sees a starry sky and another literally sees the angels of her experience who guide according to the gentle wisdom of her dear grandfather. My childhood image is an elderly man with a white beard, no doubt shown to me at some point in picture form. The holiness of my spiritual experiences in prayer lead me to see growth, to experience more mature images as well: a warm light, a masculine chest with a rose, a Picasso stained glass of Jesus, a blanket of comfort, arms holding, and the list goes on. Our mind creates tangible moments for us to savor in a spiritual experience, according to our needs and beliefs. We can meditate and pray to these same images in our weak and suffering places. We create memories of tangible healing. We grow into creation of images beautifully patterned toward individual need.

As we mature, we expand our vision of Supreme Being. James Fowler identifies three faith stages and we move out of the conventional stages rooted in childhood environments and religious establishments and into the ownership of knowing precious individual belief systems and communing with religious establishments based on discernment and experience of knowing. We mindfully are present to the most precious growth. We choose. We burst with joy of knowing and cannot help but take that out to others. Vocations and service are part of organic process of transformation through contemplation. Fowler's final stage is described as follows:

> ***Highly interpersonal. Strong emphasis on the community. Stage three believers tend to be highly involved in the community itself, accepting its values and investing energy in relating to other community members. Conventions and traditions are still important, because they contain the life of the church community (volunteers are at this stage).***
>
> – James W. Fowler, *Stages of Faith: The Psychology of Human Development*

We integrate our spirit into our life in community and service. We evoke our spirit and we celebrate through the play of creative spirit. We connect and that becomes our power as rebirthed each time we meditate and pray. The intersection of spirit and human experience leads us, as it led the man and/or spirit of Jesus Christ. Our calling becomes the *how* of our experience, lessening the priority of the *whats* that form our experience. The Benedictine Sisters note the following life changes as we walk in human experience "seeing" through the pure lens of our truth:

- Spiritual peace and harmony.
- Exhibits a notable reverence for life; an enthusiasm for life, devotion to life in all its manifestations.

- Intellectual curiosity, alertness.
- Attention to intimacy and friendship.
- Concern about prayer and reflection.
- Dedication to improving ministerial and professional skills.
- Truthful clarity of vision about self, God, others, and the world.
  - an honest and reverential approach to God, because God is Creator and Lord, Friend and Companion, Father and Mother.
  - an honest self-presentation to others, so that there is a quality of authenticity and appropriateness about personal relationships – a "what-you-see-is-what-you-get" transparency – that is deeply attractive to others.
  - a gracious acceptance and tolerance of others without denying their actual abilities and failures.
  - a similar tolerance and acceptance of self.
  - a sensibility to the grandeur of God and grace-filled reality of the world.
  - a desire to help make the world a more just and peaceful locale for all God's people.

The aforementioned is from Christian experience, my own experience of knowing. All spiritual movement and choice to becoming part of communing with others with or without religious affiliation is personal, reverent path and is to be deeply respected. We awaken our souls and behold the experience that is the dance of our life. We savor beauty and rest as Supreme Being is beholding us. We determine what we need or need do as we dwell in our hearts. We use the heartfelt experience of compassion to pray and send energy to someone or others we know in need. We touch and affect others in our Goodness. Women connect in communication and women transcendentally connect in meditation and prayer. This is feminine path. Prayer and meditation are as individually directed as snowflakes patterned in each spiritual journey. Pierre Teilhard de Chardin once said, "We are not human beings having a spiritual experience; we are spiritual beings having a human experience."

Contemplative life is walking with one foot in human experience, and one foot in spiritual experience. We listen with one ear for understanding and one ear for communing. We listen in order to see. Father Kevin Anderson states living life with opposing tensions of human and spiritual experience is represented in the *mandorla*, the Italian word for the almond-shaped intersection of two circles of opposing tensions: yin and yang, feminine and masculine, human and spirit. Contemplative life awakens us to a transcendent, sensually significant experience of living and walking in the intersection, or mandorla. Father Richard Rohr, who writes of masculine spirituality refers to this as the *liminal space.* Buddhists look to achieve what His Holiness, the Dalai Lama calls, "Individual Liberation". *Buddha* means "I am awake" in Sanskrit. We awaken, notice and allow our center to find growing edges of transformation. We live out our "something more". Our inner strength moves into our outer strength and confidence and we are affected. We shed our realities of deceit. We remove limits. We let go. We *know possiblity*. We become pure. We achieve clarity.

Clarity

C*larity* of vision effervesces into living our truest place in the world with Self-love and love of serving others. We hostess the world with our loving creations. Our *clarity* extends to loving, caring actions toward our own bodies. We protect our bodies loving energy by nurturing our Selves with pure and loving choices. I enrolled in a Reiki workshop (healing touch) with Reiki Master Tim McNamara from the Usui Center in Denver, Colorado. He spoke of the breaking down of purity and energy our society creates with it's handling and manufacturing of foods – thus denying ourselves the nurturing sustenance created by our previous generations who did not crossbreed and genetically alter food energies. Our bodies are confused and need clarity. I contrast the microwave culture of our existence with Sunday childhood meals lovingly prepared by my grandmother full of roast beef, mashed potatoes and gravy, corn on the cob and homemade buns and apple pie. I see my grandmother kneading buns, baking Norwiegian lefse and krum kaka for Christmas and my heart *knows* we cannot confuse our bodies with impure energy. I bake and cook for my children, sending them the loving memories and energy of pure nutrition hoping to create bodies of health and pure strength. I love my husband by preparing food to love his body. I listen and notice and view the lens of my human experience with spiritual love.

What if we divinely host and welcome Supreme Being into the energy of our lives? We protect our loving energy auras, filling the holes of destruction with our contemplative experience until we shine magnificently in our purest loving Truth. It's all love and it's all healing.

> ***Seeing, in the broadest and finest sense, means using your senses, your intellect, and your emotions. It means encountering your subject matter with your whole being. It means looking beyond the labels of things and discovering the remarkable world around you.***
>
> – Freeman Patterson

> ***"We are all words spoken by God and our calling is to learn how to pronounce ourselves."***
>
> – Thomas Merton

Chapter Eight

SomeOne More

Once the self is misperceived, others are misunderstood and relations become difficult. Such errors constrict the natural human sensitivity to the real concerns of the individual and others. – the Dalai Lama

Follow your bliss. – Joseph Campbell

One of my students remarked to me, "So many people with depression want to end their lives, but there's also a great many people who suffer from depression who simply want a different life – and there's such a difference." As she's telling me, I'm fondly holding her ten-month-old daughter and I know these words are unforgettable. So many simply want or need a different life and believe they have no power to create that reality. I *know* what she means instantly and then she is gone – but she's made a mark on my soul … in an instant time and space are irrelevant in our moments of connection. Ultimate knowing is immeasurable and occurs over years or in a flash. Connectedness reaches to our very core when we are open to the SomeOne Mores of our human existence. We become aware of those who bring divine *knowing* into our path.

So many people are looking for a different life and are feeling alone. Nobody chooses the realities of economic despair, illness, losing children to death and drugs and atrocities of war. Life is excruciating and we long for an alternate reality. Perhaps it is this desperation and loneliness that draws people toward the temptation of affairs. People are in such need of a third world galaxy fantasy existence void of the problematic pieces in reality. Fantasy is a misplaced attempt for a "different life" full of romance, pleasure and the thrill of falling in love. But it's not real. It's fantasy.

Affairs are harmful to self and others. My classes talk openly about the multitude of painful experiences when the infidelity is discovered. Broken trust. I spoke earlier of ethics and why we "should" choose right, but there are also reasons we "have to" choose right over wrong. In reality, there are **always** consequences. Consequences of infidelities include: self-hatred, guilt, shame, broken spirit, and distance rather than intimate personal relationship with Supreme Being. Guilt. Shame. Self-hatred. Brokenness. Affairs are betrayal of ultimate trust. Nobody ever said it was going to be easy …

As an instructor, I see the by-product – the angry children. Children who are so disappointed and confused they cannot find the love for the parent who chose happiness over them. Resentment builds, guilt and shame build and family relationships are torn and ripped and mangled. We choose to resist temptation and look to the core of our loneliness – the desire for a different life. We explore opportunity rather than destruction.

I went to an afternoon matinee of the movie *Unfaithful* a few years ago. In the movie there is a scene where a husband during his morning routine notices a sexy undergarment on a chair and pauses mid-shave to wonder. Of course, the plot revolves around his wife's affair and she's purchased the negligee for someone else. In that moment I wonder why she missed the piece of wearing sexy undergarments for her husband. And it is in that same moment I realize how little these relationships really are about great sex – they are about the fantasy and desire for a different life. A quotation from this same film is something like, "an affair has to end badly" and I deeply pondered the phrase. I'm incredibly aware of consequences, so this makes perfect sense. Rationally, if the couple ends up together, two families are destroyed. If the couple doesn't end up together, one ends it and there is pain for the other. It's like the character in *When Harry Met Sally* who keeps lamenting, "You mean you don't think he's leaving his wife?" And the friends respond (repeatedly), "No. He's never leaving his wife." Self-deception and fantasy are necessary ingredients to "believe" affairs are reality. Reality is rational and we rely on our rational thought, not our impulse. Rationally, the affair ends badly. Always. There really is no third world galaxy. Affairs are a band-aid for the deeper issue of unhappiness and/or loneliness. Affairs end. Badly.

When we want a different life, we focus on necessary changes to build one. We open ourselves to the gentle nudgings and noticings which point us toward decision-making. We stay in our Truth. We keep our spirits from brokenness and harm and remain true to self and others. We choose to do Right. We look to our community of someone mores to guide us toward wholeness and healing. We look to our someone mores to notice and celebrate the pieces of happiness in our existence. John Cougar Mellenkamp sings the lyric, "Life goes on. Long after the thrill of living is gone." I beg to differ. Ladies, we are just getting started. Our truth and connection to others and Creator as we create and re-create bring us more true joy than we can possibly fathom.

We cannot see and *know* the someone mores of our existence if we are still jaded by confusion and destructive relationships. We remove barriers and jadedness. Healthy relationships are those where we can love unconditionally and openly, giving and receiving wholeness. We use our contemplative listening to move into our hearts and listen to the people who've been brought into our lives with grandest of intention. We allow. We feel the supportive love and purpose of our intentional relationships. "Ephphatha": open up. (Mark 7:34).

Healing Relationships that "Crack us Wide Open with Pain"

Men and women who feel loss of control with life frequently move into misplaced strategies of power and control over many obsessions, and, unfortunately, even people. Sadly, many of them are full of self-deception and refusal to acknowledge the pain and loneliness they hide. Their tortured existence tries to draw love and kindness into objectified relationships. Eventually, they suck our psychological energy and wound the very love and compassion stemming from the aura of our experience. Tim McNamara, once explained our auras receive holes in negative experiences, but we have twenty-four hours to fill them back up again with love. What a great image! When I am hurt by another I spend time filling the hole with love of self and with understanding. I separate from that other in the ritual of doing so. I am not his/her story. I consciously remove myself from his/her story. Those of us who trust and give and love are sometimes reciprocated with hurt and suffering – especially by those who don't allow feeling and move into the numbness and shallowness of strategic relationships of power.

Unfortunately, I see these relationships frequently in the abusive romantic relationships my students discuss. Men and women who are into controlling others are not rational nor part of reality. *We have the power to keep our power.* We have the power to move out of his/her story. Toltec religion believes the hurt directed toward us is not even about us – it's about them, the people who are caught up in the suffering of their existence. We can cut them out of our stories just as we cut the unnecessary appendix of our body. We change the story in contemplation. We send them off in a pink ball of energy to the universe or to our God. We accept and/or forgive them for their chemical imbalance and illness, but we do not become part of the illness – we heal. We are no longer stuck, we are liberated. We remember in our authenticity and authority that we are our own power and nobody can truly have power over us, though their narratives of self-deception will continue to become the desperation and inner torture of their existence. We surround ourselves with loving relationships of health.

A student came to me in tears with the story of her abusive relationship. She bravely terminated the physically abusive relationship and rebuilt her life. I am in awe of her courage, since he allowed no support of friendships. Completely alone, she weighed the balance of her life: his needs vs. her needs, and chose power and healing. I teach her public speaking. I know, in theory, that inner confidence becomes outer confidence in speaking. I was honored and moved to watch her speak last week with a countenance of power. She exuded strength and ability and openness. I am so proud of her accomplishment and grateful for my moments of witnessing. She moved into healing friendships and personal power.

Relationships that Enchant Us: Rational and Healthy

When we look back on our lives, we see with absolute clarity the moments when others were there for us just when we needed them to be. On my first son's first birthday there was a blizzard and my relatives were literally unable to attend the party. I was incredibly disappointed until my friend, Lori, came over and tied a red ribbon around my son's one-year-old head. We watched him eat chocolate birthday cake with his fingers and smear cake and frosting all over his face. I have vivid memories of the rest of the day as well, but it's the red ribbon I most remember.

When I left for graduate school, my husband gave me a single red rose. My husband enchants me with many moments of endearment and love above all else. I look into his eyes and I see only the roses of a man who would spend the rest of his life with me.

When my car stalled on a back road before the invention of cellphones. I was left utterly alone in the cold. Just as I pondered whether to chance my fear of dogs and walk up to a farmhouse of strangers, a car pulled up. It was an elderly couple and he was on the school board of a neighboring community I knew. The couple took me into town and even made all arrangements for towing and fixing the car. I can think of no other situation where I would get into the car of a stranger and trust …

I am enchanted by those who teach. I am drawn to mentors. I see a chain of those who believed in me and led me toward knowing what I most desperately needed to know from my high school Spanish teacher, to my current conversations with Carol Ritberger. My Spanish teacher told me I'd always reach my goals, and CaroI said the healing words I already knew but needed said. I can create a mental chain of those who inspired me – and so can you.

Sometimes our someone mores bring us hope and second chances. I'm commuting with my children to their school and the further we drive the more I realize I am not prepared for the week. I've forgotten my briefcase and I don't know if my son's basketball game is at home or away and I should have preset the oven for the chicken we're having for dinner. Finally, I make a decision. Since I have no early morning appointments I can go home and start over. I drop off the children, drive home, grab my briefcase, check the game schedule and preset the oven. There. I am ready. I've been given a second chance.

Recently, I had a chance to examine second chances at a much deeper level. I was scheduled to present at the National Communication Association Conference in Boston. I was honored to be presenting a paper and a panel this year. As the days drew near, I spent hours perfecting presentations and making social plans with instructors I hadn't seen in years. The day before we were to fly to Boston, I woke up with a rhythmic pain in my right side. I'd felt it during the night as well and was starting to become concerned. I pictured the organs on the right side of the body and concluded it might be my appendix. I ended up at a clinic, an imaging center, and finally the hospital – with a diagnosis of … appendicitis. It's amazing the way life happens and we are absolutely out of control in moments such as this. I was supposed to be having a "girl's weekend" with my dear friend and co-author, Erin, and integrating phenomenal amounts of professional inspiration. Instead I was on a gurney in the hospital with my husband holding my hand as I cried tears of utter disappointment and fear. I was crushed. That was only the beginning because there were complications. By the time I was released, I knew I had been part of a miracle. I have a second chance at life … a second chance to be whomever I want. We can create all possibility because miracles occur all of the time and bring us hope. We are all in a state of healing and our someone mores guide the process.

Laughter is healing. Friends bring us laughter and laughter is healing. My friend Patty says, "now the only appendix you have is at the back of this book." Elizabeth, a writer, came over with just what I needed: the gem of true friendship and the gem of a navel ring! I hadn't been able to reinsert my navel piercing ring after surgery, which devastated the rebellious part of my nature. Elizabeth knows me. I need to show the world my refusal to accept and become part of what the world says I *should* be … and the ring symbolically does just that. She stayed and we talked about all sorts of important spiritual perceptions. I admire her depth and openness.

We discussed everyone's ability to connect spiritually with mentors who inspire. We gently lift them down from pedestals and place them beside us. They have greatness and so do we. It's in our true path of power. We create circles of people and mental/spiritual connection. I image them smiling and draw psychological energy and limitless meaning in the image. Consider the infinite possibility of that concept – we can invite Einstein, Oprah, and Dalai Lama into our circle of spiritual connectedness. Conversations with Elizabeth allow possibility and I find myself searching into the depths of my soul to respond. She listens, we laugh, and feel sadness as I recount the story of my surgery and healing. She asks, "But what do you *know*? What do you *know* for sure?"

I found myself responding in such power. Unbelievably I was verbalizing abstractions, thoughts and nuances of my intuitive reading of the experience as the epiphany it was. I *knew* in the hospital that with my renewed health and experience, I would focus only on my writing and spiritual work toward women and healing. I would reject any barriers – especially the unfocused academic writing and numerous networking opportunities I'd immersed myself in previous to the attack as necessary components toward building a business and increasing our finances. My verbal response represented the streamlined clarity of vision I received as I lay in a hospital bed and sorted through tears. I *know* I am *only and honorably* to concern myself with the healing and empowering of women. During my conversation with Elizabeth, abstractions became concrete thought and action. Elizabeth connected my mind, body, and spirit that day. Such gift. Elizabeth is someone more. Someone mores in our lives bring abstract beliefs into concrete reality of the stories and perceptions we choose to surround us in as we move through life's path in a loving, healing manner. We are gently and lovingly guided.

When we look upon life we see we are enchanted by people in our lives because they are brought to us in just the right time and in just the right manner to be a part of us. Sometimes we learn from them as mentors, sometimes we learn from them in our suffering, and sometimes we live life to its fullest with them in our fun and our daring adventures. We are enchanted by others because *we are meant to* live stories of beauty and enchantment.

SomeOne More: Beyond Rational

Sometimes I intuit moments of profound connection and I am astounded. The synchronicity and common understanding seems to prevail even and especially in moments without words. The more we move out of our heads and into our hearts to listen, the more we return to our head with a perception of deep connection to those in our lives. We are restored with psychological energy to send out in gift to others. Spirit connects. I allow my spirit to speak to the spirits of my mentors in prayer. I allow movement and growth of my own being to know my giftedness because of their vision. We connect and there is the power inspiring my writing as the very lights and flickerings join to illuminate the world in feminine healing, love and compassion, and power.

I am praying in a Catholic hospital room and a Chaplain is praying the words I'm unable to express. I envision Mary when I'm in need of comfort. I only recently chose my particular religion, which is why I can openly appreciate other's individual choices. Years before I chose my religion I read about the Marian apparitions in the world with intense intrigue. I've never learned to pray the rosary, but have recently been reading about it. The Chaplain closes her prayer with, "Hail Mary, full of grace …" and I'm overcome with emotion because of a memory from long ago.

I'm looking at the pupil of the eye. I am intrigued by the pupil because it cannot be rationally explained. I am seventeen and am in the Basilica in Mexico City viewing the relic of something beyond explanation. The miracle is told by Robert Ellsberg:

> ***On the morning of December 9, 1531, a Christian Indian named Juan Diego was on his way to Mass. As he passed a hill at Tepeyac, not far from present-day Mexico City, he heard a voice calling him by name. Looking up he was surprised to see a young Indian maiden. She instructed him to go to the bishop and tell him to construct a church on this hill, the site of an ancient Nahuatl shrine to the mother goddess. Juan faithfully carried out the assignment, but the bishop paid him no attention. In subsequent showing the maiden charged him to try again,***

> ***this time identifying herself as the Mother of God. Again, the bishop scoffed. At a third audience with the Lady, she instructed Juan Diego to gather a bouquet of roses which were growing, unseasonably, at her feet. Juan gathered the roses in his tilma or cape. Having gained another audience with the bishop, who had demanded some kind of sign, Juan Diego opened his tilma to present the flowers. To his astonishment, he discovered a full-color image of the Lady mysteriously imprinted on the rough fabric.***

It is 1978 and I'm standing in front of holiness – Juan Diego's tilma. The pupil beholds an imprint of Juan's reflection upon seeing her. The imprint of Juan is too small to be humanly painted or created – the miracle of *beyond rational.* I am transfixed. Others gather in pilgrimage and light votive candles of love and hope and faith. I am immersed in a world of holiness expressed in the ladder of flames ascending in pyramids of love toward statues of the Sainted Virgin. The faith is transparent and transcendent through the actions of genuflection, crawling, kneeling, and adorations of kisses. There is no noise, only silence. But there are sounds, glorious nuances of prayer and healing being chanted. "Hail Mary, full of grace. Blessed art thou among women and blessed be the fruit of the womb, Jesus." And I am among women. I am among all who adore. I envision all miracles of Mary and grasp the perfection and blessedness of moments like this which encapture the light of Grace. Words are helpless, only symbolic. Illumination such as this shines deeply. It can only be experienced, impassioned, awakened – penetrating deeper than real form or substance. Ecstatic knowing.

The Chaplain completes her prayer and I open my eyes to my hospital room and present experience. The pale, olive paint was dull, but is now illuminated as are all objects within my visual focus. I turn to the chaplain and see so much more than only a few minutes ago in rational time. Previously, I saw a woman dedicated to helping others heal. I now see a woman who knew just the right prayer to connect me with Supreme Being in just the right way for my present spiritual path. I see her only in her holiness. I see her ability to *take me there* – where I want to be, with my God. She has become someone more.

After my mother died, I remained close to her parents. Eventually, my grandmother was left alone and moved into a nursing home. I continued to visit her and love her. As her physical health began to deteriorate in later years, she would have days that were difficult. She rarely complained, and I always tried to sense what she needed or was able to do. Some days I played piano for her, and one day we sang loudly in the visitation chairs of the courtyard a song that exemplifies her ability to remain positive:

Oh what a beautiful morning,
Oh what a beautiful day.
I've got a beautiful feeling
Everything's going my way.
– Rodgers & Hammerstein, *Oklahoma!*

Another day she spoke to me of a long-ago boyfriend and the response of my grandfather to the attention of another and I remembered the way he lovingly attended to her and taught her finances in elder years to prepare her if he died first. I felt fortunate to listen to her speak of her life. She told me of the voice lessons she was denied and I remembered her dedication to church choir for years of her adult life. She spoke to me of her courtship with my grandfather with a pearl necklace for the engagement and a dozen roses for the wedding. I remembered the voices of both grandparents praying the Lord's Prayer each night when we were all in bed – and I knew they held hands as they prayed because I once saw. I remember only love from my visits to their farm where we climbed silos and did somersaults in haylofts and walked around graves of the Six Mile Grove Country Church reading tombstones of those who'd gone before trying to guess their stories. Although she is now a tombstone and a beautiful story, I mostly remember her final visits when she would remark, "Why am I as close to you as I am my own daughter?" I said then what I knew and what I still know, "Because it's just love. It's that simple." We knew how to magnificently move into only love and let go of all else. When my appendectomy was complete, my surgeon told me he'd never had such a small incision or "easy" surgery. My prayers brought images of my mother and my grandmother's hands helping him as someone mores who still protect and guide. I laughed when I discovered his name was clearly Norwegian as it resonated within my multitude of memories of Norwegian speaking during Christmas secrets and holidays of krum kaka, lefse, and rosettes. My grandmother and mother and he together became someone more toward my miracle of healing.

Walking the mandorla of spiritual and human existence also brings us ageless souls. Let me tell you about Emily who was born with a mature soul. I've known Emily more than twelve years. As young children, Emily, her brother and my boys played with energy and laughter. Such wonderful fun for themselves running from room to room re-enacting the boardgame "Clue" with pretend murder weapons and trying to outguess each other. A couple of years later, they decided to start a newspaper. They met at the coffee shop each week for much of the summer dividing up responsibilities and planning. During summers we met at the beach weekly for more than ten years. We used to laugh that we'd be doing beach days for so many years they'd eventually be driving themselves there. And they are. The toddlers who played on the slide and swings on breaks from splashing now lay on towels and swim and, well, put sand in each other's hair. Genuine fun. It's rare for children in our current society of noise and busyness to find these genuine moments of laughter. We laugh until our sides hurt and our cheeks ache. I spoke with Emily, now seventeen, on the phone a few nights ago and we are still laughing – in this case because of the story of my appendectomy and incision, which hurt every time I laughed. But she owed me that.

About ten years ago, our family was visiting Emily in the Children's Hospital because she had just had surgery to remove a cancerous tumor. We tried so desperately not to make her laugh, and, yet, that was always the nature of our relationship. So as families talked and tried to be there for Emily, she was constantly squeezing her morphine drip to ease the pain of the laughter. I see her so vividly in that moment and it still seems unbelievable.

Norm Cuzins cured his cancer through laughter therapy. Well, it certainly seemed worth pursuing, besides we were in the midst of a horrid tornado season and my own children needed to relax. We spent that summer focused on laughter, fun, and listening to Emily's needs and accepting her in all of her various physical conditions as she treated the remaining parts of her body into wellness. Norm Cuzins did so much with his influence – and so did Emily. I hesitate to tell you of her illness, because in my eyes she never was her *illness*, she was always her *wellness*. Emily is the inspiration of my own desire to know healing for all who are in need. Emily was only nine, and still she knew intuitively what I discuss in later chapters. I want you to picture Emily in wellness.

Once, Emily stayed overnight during a week of swimming lessons the children took together. At the time, her hair had come out because of chemotherapy treatments. That night, at dinner, she told me of a naïve and, therefore, insensitive girl at the pool who had bluntly asked, "Why do you have no hair? Why on earth would you do that?" I'll never forget her response the following day. She rubbed vaseline all over her head and shook glitter on it. Then she simply said, "There. Now I'll really give her something to ask about." They say life is 10% what happens and 90% how we react to it. Emily knew how to react to it.

Amazingly, Emily was struck with a second form of cancer a few years later. Again, her intellect/body/emotions/spirit joined together in community with others and prayer toward the power of healing. Emily is wellness. Now Emily is involved in so many high school activities, many of them in voluntary and leadership positions. She is preparing for college and is involved in the most beautiful romantic relationship. Although we tease her about "the boy", we are all touched by the happiness she is presently receiving – and she deserves to savor all of it. My desire is for her to always be lavished in happiness and laughter and love and healing. She's the one who continues to make *me* laugh and help *me* heal. Serendipitous circle of healing.

When we focus on the moments of kindness brought to us in so many unique ways meant only to be perfectly for us, we can be awestruck of the existence of Higher Good and much grander picture of our own path in life. We can truly visualize a path that winds and finds and shifts and moves toward happiness, connection and ultimate joy. We see moments of complacency, suffering, pain amidst a path which is also full of kindnesses and Graces – if we take notice. *Knowing* prepares us and comforts us in our present times and needs with Timeless Clarity and Compassion. We become unstuck and move into a walk of Noticing and Becoming.

The snowflakes are tiny crystals that don't register as snow on our complex and technologically developed weather equipment. Yet the crystals continue to fall, secretly and brilliantly. I'm driving. Doorlocks automatically lock as if to protect me from the dangers of the road. The analogy moves me instantly back to the wonderful massage I've just received at a Women's Spirituality Farm named Clare's Well. The ending of the massage always brings me just to the brink of sleep, yet in my almost slumber I am prayerfully noticing the hands of my healing and the vessel of my God's love the masseur becomes. The experience is what my friend calls "ethereal" – and I'm feeling the honor of the ethereal connection as her fingertips move to close my energy into a pale pink shield of protectiveness. My incision burns with the passion of closure and wellness. My body calmly allows open chakras, open energy and open thought. "I am healed" surprises me as thought, though it was my intent. And I *know* I am well. And I *know* the ethereal connection of Aggie who is *SomeOne More* for so many who carry the burdens of illness and stress.

Delight in the wisdom of noticing given pleasures. Enjoy the delights of people who surround us as intended by a Supreme Being who deeply and unconditionally loves. Marvel at how many times you've instantaneously, timelessly, and deeply been the *SomeOne More* just in the right moment for another's path. Lovingly, we give with intent to Love.

> ***Let us get arrogance out of our lives, the conceit, the egotism. Let us be more compassionate, gentler, filled with more forbearance, patience, forgiveness, and a greater measure of respect for one another.***
> – Gordon B. Hinckley, leader of the LDS Church

> ***a spiritual life also promises something more radical, in the true sense of the word: that is going to the root, the core. Spirituality offers the possibility that we can actually become free from the destructive energy of a stressed out life. Spirituality promises a kind of simplicity in the midst of our complex world.***
> – Brian Taylor, *Becoming Human*

Chapter Nine

Intuited Selflessness: The Joy of Mothering

When you are a mother, you are never really alone in your thoughts. You are connected to your child and to all those who touch your lives. A mother always has to think twice, once for herself and once for her child. – Sophia Loren

"Each day through my childhood I would bend down to the feet of my father and mother and kiss them. This is a practice in my culture which is dying, but it has so much value for me. It is a means of honoring the father and mother. Now that I am grown and here in America to attend college, I miss that. I wish I could see my mother and father and honor them with a practice I many times took for granted."

I am deeply touched by the woman's words to my class and I wish, also, that she could afford to visit her parents back in Sri Lanka. I am touched by the opportunity of intuitively knowing a mother who sacrificed the heartfelt missing of her child to provide what is best for her – an education. I ask the student later if she will raise her own children with the precious honoring of her culture, and she responds instantly--she will. The honoring of her father and mother is her deepest value.

Women intuitively mother. Whether we choose to literally become mothers or to figuratively care for the children of our world in other meaningful ways, we are graced with the knowing of how to connect, how to care for, how to see a vision of future goodness and know our place within it. We move into becoming SomeOne More to children. It's human nature to leave something of our richest gift behind, whether it be artwork, writings, meaningful projects or volunteering, donating or true miracle of birthing to continue our character, our value, our love when we are gone. Spiritual truth and deepest knowing of self through discernment guide us through mournings of lost children and miscarriages, choices to bring children into the world as gift, and createdness of nurturing through figurative concern for world in our own choice to heal and to love. My heart aches for those who wish to mother and physically cannot. My prayer is for discernment and opportunity to heal, to love, to mother in unique, different manner. We leave our very best behind. We live knowing our truth and it is the divine truth of our souls that is gently placed upon the earth.

The glory of mothering is sometimes overwhelmingly hidden with messages of our popular culture of noise and technology. Further, we seek harmony and balance with the fear that prevails in our hearts and minds from daily messages and conversations of destruction and death brought to us through the many vehicles of our media. Our world is quickly changing and challenging us to step up and create the balance. We are called to simplicity and love. We are called to the someone more of our being to restore the balance of love and connection in a world of seeming disconnect. We mother literally and figuratively with feminine spirit of connection.

Joni Mitchell and the Counting Crows sang the same message to audiences decades apart who chose to savor the simplicity and purity of paradise. The culture of the seventies wanted more than the decisions of establishment – they cherished authentic, pure world. Decades later, the compact disc "Hardy Candy" in 2002 echoed the surprise of a message … with an unlisted song for those lucky enough to notice – a gift, as it were. The gift of a message calling us to protect and savor our world and the paradise of our children's future:

Don't it always seem to go
That you don't know what
You've got till it's gone
They paved paradise
And put up a parking lot
– Big Yellow Taxi

Discernment speaks of the paradise of pure earth and creation. Discernment speaks passionately of the paradise of our children. We cannot wait any longer to save our earth and our children with necessary messages of love. Truly, we are called to determine what we can leave behind to make our world better. We nurture, intuitively knowing and intuitively creating the simplicity and balance needed by children in a world moving too fast to remain authentic and whole. The rhythm of life lies in a balance of knowing fear and destruction, but responding as necessary. We choose coping and model loving stories of comfort and safety. We protect. We are called to be selfless. We are called to pay attention and respond to current messages and stories in our media that tip the scale for children in our culture with way too many narratives of worry and fear.

Media Induced Fear

When interference occurs with heartfelt love of mothering, it is felt in our very bones. Mothers give and sacrifice as they discover astonishing levels of giving and sacrifice. I am proud of the children I have brought into this world and I propel them into the world of their createdness. The gift of reciprocated unconditional love and acceptance moves me to deepest gratitude. I know I will protect – at any cost. Even sacrificing my life. Children present opportunity to know our deepest, loving, giving self. Children provide opportunity for our giving.

No woman would allow a violent stranger to come into her home, yet most of us do so almost daily with television. Television has changed since we were young. The black and white images were incapable of showing red blood, and were far less "real". We currently have news shows sensationalizing events with stories, and fantasy or non-fiction shows (particularly police and courtroom genre) attempting to appear "real". The line between fantasy and reality is most definitely blurred and we are losing sight of what is best for loving development of children. Despite my attempts at shielding my young boys from mature content in the media, they still were exposed to conversation and images of O.J. Simpson's trial and Bill Clinton's infidelities ... in detail I was relieved they didn't yet have intellectual development to comprehend.

Mothers protect – even when in fear. When September 11th occurred I was dropping my Schitzu off at the groomer's and the woman and I stared at the small black and white television in the corner of her shop unable to take in what we were seeing. I drove the few miles back home trying to sort, to feel, to get some rational interpretation. Ironically, this was my first day working from home--ever. Instead of savoring the pleasure of realizing the dream, I was visibly shaken and making decisions to ensure the safety of my own children. When the water softener man came to deliver bags of salt, he remarked, "Did you hear they almost got the Pentagon now?" Then he left. And I was alone.

All of us recall with vivid detail the sensory images of the **moment we knew** of the attack, the moment we realized we were helplessly out of control of our reality and we were anesthetized in fear. The paralysis evolved into chaotic retort: political image, angry defense, misplaced blame of cultures, and frightful images and stories left for our innocence to sort. Repeated images and stories forced their way into our cognition, waiting for us to critically sort according to our value systems. Only we couldn't critically sort the attack into our value systems because it was no part of anything we believed in

– only hate and evil. As we replayed the story time and time again trying to make sense of the happening, the media replayed the story time and time again shoving evil and hate images and narratives into our conscious, our subconscious, and our unconscious, anesthetized beings. And covers of magazines showed graphic images of fire, destruction, death and lay on coffee tables, rugs, and countertops for all of our children to see and to see and to see.

Somewhere a three year old girl asked her mother, "why did a plane fall on a building?" An odd e-mail was circulating claiming Nostradamus had predicted the attack, with promises of further apocalyptic happenings. A third grade teacher was reprimanded in central Minnesota for sharing the e-mail with her class. All were encompassed in fear.

This wasn't the first occurrence of children watching tragedy unfold. In 1986 the world viewed the Challenger disaster. An article in *Journal of Communication* states, "Reports that 25% of 5-8 year olds, 48% of 9-13 year olds, and 31% of 14-17 year olds saw the shuttle launch and explosion live at school." My colleague and friend, Dr. Erin Szabo and I joined together researching and writing in hope of helping our unprotected children. The only previous research Erin and I saw studied the effects of the Challenger disaster and the war in Iraq. Eerily, in the short time we wrote our first paper, the Columbia exploded and we went to war with Iraq. We watched, in horror, as Saturday morning television was interrupted on all channels, except one, in our cable network to give a play-by-play of the Columbia disaster. We imagined children expecting cartoons and seeing disaster.

Television news is perceived as real, thus removing any coping thought of "it can't really happen". Instead, we watch nightmares unfold. Recent statistics show kidnapping constituting less than 2% of all violent crimes against children under eighteen, and most of these are custody disputes. The AACAP in 2002 reported a decrease in crime in the U.S., but an increase in news reporting crime of 240%! And children are watching television news, many on a daily basis as they eat dinner or in the evening before bed. Neilson ratings suggest around a half million children between the ages of two and eleven are watching the evening news daily. Children are even required to watch the news for classroom assignments in current events and global issues.

Children growing up in fear are in divided energy and are limited or prevented from experience of joy in childhood. Calm is necessary for holistic development. Certainly, fear is not inevitably bad. Fear is self-protective and even energizing or fun, but it can also be debilitating and interfere with normal, necessary healthy behaviors of sleeping, eating, learning, concentrating, and developing trusting relationships. Children and adults need healthy coping to balance the barrage of fear created by all vehicles of technology in current culture. We have a need to know about our world, but we do not have a need to be constantly exposed to narratives of fear, death, destruction, and hopelessness. We are allowing the media to shape the narratives of our reality. Further, we certainly don't need to become part of a narrative that believes war is done in the name of a Christian God.

Age-Appropriate Triggers and Coping

Before I give a brief synopsis of what we learned through our research, I would like to recommend the book *Mommy, I'm Scared* by Joanne Cantor. She and others have created the work we intend to continue. Joanne Cantor was an educator at the University of Wisconsin in Madison. Since I'm an educator, it makes sense to me to follow children's fright reaction triggers in a developmental method also used to understand development of learning. The method is Piaget's Theory of Cognitive Development. Cantor suggests cognitive development may influence comprehension of television content, social reality perceptions, and fright responses (1998). This framework creates an understanding of how children understand the world, predictions of potential fright triggers, and age-appropriate coping strategy. Fears don't develop in a linear pattern. In other words, we keep some fears, resolve others, and new ones are formed. We are not always conscious of our fears. In fact, many **adults** still sleep with covers over their feet to subconsciously protect their toes from the monster under the bed!

The first stage of cognitive development is *preoperational* (ages 2-7). The next is *concrete operational* (ages 8-12), and finally, *formal operational* (ages 13 and over). *Preoperational* thought is best classified by a tendency to focus mainly on highly visual cues in the environment, and a propensity to attend to only one striking feature of an object. Also, these young children have a difficult time separating fantasy from reality. Images of Bin Laden as "a bad man" would be particularly bothersome. *Images* frighten, not intent or realistic threat.

Concrete thought is more mature, thus children are more frightened of realistic threats. Realistic, frightening news events should be bothersome to children in this stage, because they recognize the event poses a potential threat. Further, there's an overestimation the event could occur. Cantor recognizes for children ages ten and up, another property of media presentations responsible for inducing emotional stress is the *perceived possibility* that the portrayed event could happen (1988). We surveyed a small, central Minnesota town and discovered similar media-induced fright response to research done in Santa Barbara, California. In other words, though the Santa Barbara children were exposed to higher crime in a major city, the small town, central Minnesota children perceived themselves as likely to be involved in realistic violence – thus illustrating an overestimated perception of possibility.

Cantor uses *The Incredible Hulk* to illustrate distinctions between younger children (*preoperational*) and older children (*concrete operational*). When the Hulk turns into the big, green strong monster to help victims, he becomes a frightful image for younger children.

Just before the actor, Bill Bixby, turns into the Hulk would be more frightening to older children. For example, if a victim is in a fire and needs the Hulk's help, it's the situation of the fire creating a fright trigger for *concrete operational* stage.

Formal operations stage begins about age thirteen and continues into adulthood. Thoughts are no longer tied to observable events, it allows for more abstract, logical, and formal thinking. People use analytical, hypothetical and deductive reasoning. It's argued only 50-60% of adults fully achieve this level of cognitive development.

Our survey of 174 third through ninth graders in 2001 fit Piaget's Theory of Cognitive Development. We weren't able to survey younger children of preoperational stage, like the young girl who lamented the image of the plane falling on the building, though her vivid image remains with her each time they fly and she asks, "And we'll be okay if we fly in this plane?" When we asked children to respond with description of images/stories that frightened them from television news or news magazine programs from the past year, we received many disturbing comments. Unfortunately, we found the suspected media-induced fear. At one point, we almost stopped because our hearts were breaking as we read results. We found media-induced fright from violent images, "realistic" portrayals, and abstract concepts. Here are some of the children's comments (spelling and grammar of children intact):

Examples of Violent/crime images

- "I think it was scary when they show people killing their own kids or biting someone up with a bat." (Eight year old male).
- "The Columbia Tragedy because they found body parts – that grossed me out." (Eight year old female).
- "There were people shoting other people and having people setting of boms." (Nine year old male).
- "Wen thay show wen the pepel cil pepel" (ie., When they show when the people kill people). (Nine year old female).

Examples of Violence or Crime

- "Cold Spring shootings and other shootings." (Fifteen year old male).

Examples of Personal Vulnerability

- "I was scared by mreder, because I'm afrad that I will be mredred." (Nine year old male).
- "On the news I saw a picture of a bomb in Iraq and it scared me but part of it is I have been scared to be home alone. P. S. September 11☹" (Nine year old female).

Older children's and adolescent's fear of victimization demonstrated a higher level of **abstract** thinking:

- "I was watching the interview on Elizabeth Smart. She had just been returned from that guy and I started thinking, "What if I was stolen, possibly raped and gone from friends and family for more than two years?" (eleven year old female).
- "When I hear that iraq may have biological wepons and that they might lunch them at the U.S." (Twelve year old male).

Our nation's children have cognitive "internal architecture" of fear … realities consisting of narratives of fear. Each time we fail to converse with our children about what they are viewing, we are nonverbally sending messages children view as approval and acceptance. We cannot nurture children while allowing images and stories of destruction, despair, and hopelessness. We are creating a culture of dis-ease and mistrust and fear. Children and adults need cognitive thought and experience of coping, calm, and love. One young girl is losing touch with her ability to love and to trust:

> ***When anyone gets kidnapped or raped, it scares me because I'm always alone in the mornings and I think someone is gonna break into my house and try to rape or kidnap me. It scares me a lot, because I'm never safe. And I saw a news channel one night talking about date rape***

and that scares me too, and I'm scared to get serious in any relationship." – 14-year-old female

We are called to respond.

Since the fright triggers for younger children are visual, the visual coping strategy is appropriate. Young children can be easily distracted and comforted with drinks of water, stuffed animals and blankets, food, hugs. More importantly, though young children cannot control the frightful image, they can have control (inner power) through response. Every young child should be taught control reaction of leaving the room, turning off the television, and changing the channel. Every young child deserves tools to recognize physical reactions to fear and steps to prevent further exposure.

Older children should be encouraged to think about the fear stimulus in a different light. Because of *perceived possibility*, the child should be taught to convince one's self the event is unlikely to happen, perhaps listing five or ten reasons why the event is unlikely to happen. The importance of fear should not be minimized. We live in a culture that sees fear as a weakness and children learn to repress fears. Fear is a normal part of human experience for all ages. It's a myth fear goes away as we get older. Validating the fear is reassuring–especially if listening to an older child tell about frightening events.

Mostly, as Cantor suggests, "The best approach is to provide her with the information and tools that will help her prevent it from happening, or at least that will make her feel more in control of the situation or its outcome (Cantor, 1998, p. 150). One of our survey comments by a fourteen year old female was, "Pretty much things I can't control scare me." Coping strategy should include communicating protection and power through security measures and building self-worth to handle, and means of controlling *reaction* to fear. Since there is an unbalance of fantasy/reality in television programming, we need to especially emphasize elements of a personal nature that protect the child.

Again, the cognitive shaping needs to be strong with connectors of calm and love. As I ran amidst occassional snowflakes this morning I saw a frozen pond with a name shoveled in the snow across enough ice to be seen from the house in the distance. I wondered which child could peer out the window and see the name of who she is proudly announced to the world. Children, and adults alike, need loving confidence of who they are and who they are in life's truest path. Too many children and adults make decisions against healing because of fear. They don't trust true spirit because they've no recognition or cognition to rely on in difficult moments. Creating new stories is creating the very connection/communion spirit needs in intellect to move into wholeness.

Narrative therapy is often used with children who have detachment disorder. The children go through intense therapy, including touch and holding, but they simultaneously create narratives of loving parents. The emotional scar remains, but the reaction moves out of the painful and into the loving. Our nation owns a scar, but we choose a response of moving into womanhood of protection and mothering. Mothering involves assessment of values as displayed in media, voicing of wrongs being shown, and touching and holding our nation's children every way we can.

Even our nation's current view of touch is disconcerting. As a communication instructor I know touch as a reinforcer of messages, an accent to compliment an empathic moment, and a symbol of the needed affection. Further, all humans need touch. Infants deprived of touch develop detachment disorder. Children deprived of touch aren't learning skills to be in loving relationships. Adolescents deprived of love turn to sexual behavior rather than hugs. As a mother of two teenage boys I'm aware of what we teach in our culture, and teenage boys are taught to be embarrassed of motherly hugs and kisses – though dating and sexual affection is applauded. We continue to love our children every way we can. No mother should ever deny a child hugs and lavished attention. No woman should ignore any child's fear or anger. Our nation statistically touches less than many other cultures. Legally, we've now created words to protect women and children which ironically also prevent the exact thing they crave – affection and touch. We've successfully removed any capacity to touch or to hug without legal repercussions. We search for new ways to figuratively touch, to show caring. Children are in fear, and children need hugs, holding, and loving.

As a mother, I once turned to the advice of a therapist. At the time, we were suffering devastating tornado destruction in our area and one of my children was increasingly anxious as all television coverage and social conversation replayed a narrative of fear in his second grade mind. We sat on our front porch in wicker viewing sky blue and sun and he said, "Mommy, I know it's nice out and I still can't quit being scared of the tornadoes." And so I sought help to restore the balance and I was blessed to discover a therapist who balanced his need to feel fear for survival with his need to feel safe in our world. She restored the health of my most precious child. Years later, I'm still expressing gratitude and admiration of her healing with children. We remember the rhythm of life: to feel fear or confusion, yet the balance of coping and love brings us back to our safety and deepest calm existence. Clearly, in the case of a tornado, our fear is what allows us to survive, to take cover. Fear is necessary, but so are coping tools and necessary stories of love and calm to find balance in the child. The therapist we worked with became one of my SomeOne Mores. Carol has such exquisite stories of moving children from fear into love.

Carol Leinonen, Psy.D., a licensed psychologist, incorporates animal therapy. The beauty of her work is that animals are able to shower loving affection on children in need, even when humans won't or can't. Her past dog, Smokey, and her current dog, Tanya both have sat with many children as they wept. The dogs lick tears from faces and wait on laps of children with the patience of knowing when the sadness is complete. Dogs unconditionally love. My own Schitzu nuzzles the feet of the one in need, and counts and searches each evening for all family members to return home. Tanya follows intuition as guide toward healing others. Tanya especially helps young children who fear monsters.

Dogs are healing children. Remember young children don't distinguish fantasy from reality, so the monsters under their beds and in their closets are quite real. The same perception allows the child to believe new stories of calm and coping. A young girl was afraid of vampires. Under the guidance of Carol, the young girl drew a picture of her named fear, the vampire, on a small piece of paper. Carol told her the story of Tanya, who didn't like monsters because they frightened children and made them sad. In fact, when Carol asked Tanya, "What do we do with naughty monsters?" and showed her the paper, the dog grabbed the paper and chewed it to pieces. The girl was delighted and relieved and they threw away the paper. In fact, they practiced with bigger and bigger pieces of paper, and Tanya responded with even stronger dislike as her entire being pawed and chewed and ripped until there was nothing left of the vampire on the paper. And the little girl laughed and hugged Tanya. The child was given a picture of Tanya to keep near her bed, and she slept in peace, knowing she was protected by the dog who dislikes vampires. So many other children know Tanya and keep drawn pictures or photos near beds, and sleep in calm and peace. Tanya loves and touches.

Carol also owns Bobby, a Quarterhorse-Morgan cross. A young boy once needed attention and love, and Bobby responded. The boy was small and unable to bridle the horse and Bobby responded. Once the boy saddled the horse, Bobby would actually bow his head to allow the boy to reach to place the bridle. Bobby did not do this for anyone but the boy. The horse intuited the boy's truth. Also, when the boy wanted to mount the horse, Bobby would actually tip his body to the left, thus lowering the stirrup. Did Bobby, the horse, cognitively know it lowered a stirrup? Of course not. But Bobby and Tanya know what many people don't yet know, the ability to follow intuition and unconditionally love those in need.

The final story I know of Carol's work includes a story told to her as a child by her mother. When she was frightened of the dark, her mother would ask her to imagine how many angels could fit in the bedroom. There were so many angels in the room taking care of her, they couldn't even have room to unfold their wings. And Carol slept peacefully with images of angels and love and caring. As do the children who know Carol.

Mothers who are aware of spirit and truth trust intuition and listen to nurturing guidance to create new stories. The stories of love balance the horrid stories presented in our culture. Children sleep peacefully and move into healthy development of being loved. Unconditional love and healthy mothering prevent misplaced addictions.

Addictions anesthetize the fear, but don't heal the fear. Children and adults in fear may give up. Years later, adults find themselves reacting to distress with quite immature coping because the brain never grew in it's coping synapses – only the irrational synapses of paralysis and distraction grew stronger. Healing is daring to focus energy and thought toward coping growth. Cognitively, we create coping, loving stories. Spiritually, we create memories of knowing through our contemplation with the most precious of all loving stories. Growth of spirit is channeled energy, not dissipated sparks of attempt.

Without appropriate response, pain of struggle weakens the spirit – may even break the spirit. Joan Chittester remarks in her book *Scarred by Stuggle, Transformed by Hope*, "it is not struggle that defeats us, it is our failure to struggle that depletes the human spirit." We're all aware of life's ability to be unpredictable. Children and adults without appropriate coping behaviors can become the children who "fail to struggle", who "give up". Children and adults alike are anesthetizing themselves with prescription drugs, illegal drugs, alcohol because they don't have cognitive images and experiences of calm, peace and love to balance the barrage of noise and violence.

Achieving wellness is balancing perceptions of pain with perceptions of love and knowing.

As children, we honor our mothers and fathers with daily kisses at their feet of blessing and love. We are blessed because we live in gratitude of knowing we are breathing from day to day with purpose of the truth of our existence. We honor the children in our lives touching them any and every way we can. We heal them with our simplicity, our love, and our intuitive knowing the giftedness we individually can leave them when our bodies no longer breathe, but our soul gently, lovingly lingers on. We don't know what we've got until it's gone – cherish the children. Save Paradise.

> ***I did not have my mother long, but she cast over me an influence which has lasted all my life. The good effects of her early training I can never lose. If it had not been for her appreciation and her faith in me at a critical time in my experience, I should never likely have become an inventor. I was always a careless boy, and with a mother of different mental calibre, I should have turned out badly. But with her firmness, her sweetness, her goodness, were potent powers to keep me in right path. My mother was the making of me. The memory of her will always be a blessing to me.*** – Thomas Edison

Chapter Ten

The Pleasure of Healing

When the mind is stable, feelings are forgotten.
When the body is immaterial, energy circulates.
When the mind dies, the spirit lives.
When positivity is strong, negativity vanishes.
These are the natural patterns. – Taoist meditation

There's nothing quite so beautiful as cross country skiing at twilight. The full moon illuminates the sky while warm, yellow luminescent bags lit by a single flame light a winding trail through trees, wooden bridges and silouettes of evergreens, spruce, and quiet. I stand with cold on my cheeks and sweat beneath my arms from an hour journey comprised of uphill bird-like climb and downhill surprises of speed in darkness, risk, and laughter. The flat terrain is full of conversation and charming calm of nature. I fall, but Patty helps me up, though it takes quite sometime amidst my own embarrassment and laughter. Denise brings me a pale blue scarf that suits my coat perfectly because it bothers her I never wear scarves in winter. I wrap the scarf and find it, admittingly, quite cozy and soft on my skin. I'm thankful for an evening of play. Play is incredibly spiritual and necessary. Daring to coast down hills of darkness trusting only grooves of trails to hold skis while candles cannot provide clarity is a letting go, of sorts. I shout with glee, childlike, as the fun of the speed invigorates me. Pure fun.

Later, I'm indulging in the pleasure of the most wonderful treat for myself. I'm eating bruschetta and the crunchy toast points dipped in olive oil and vinegar blend with intuited amounts of swirls of basil and garlic as the sour/sweet tomato and mozzarella cause ecstatic dancing among tastebuds amidst cacophony of delight. Generous mouthfuls of spicy cabernet sauvignon from Chile intermingle and I completely, blissfully, relax in the moment. I am celebrating. I am celebrating opportunity and my husband and I toast to hopes and adventures that are appearing and lining up in our lives so perfectly, like candles in luminescent bags showing us the next steps of our journey together. Momentary recent setbacks in my health are forgotten as I focus on newfound truth: we create our own realities and heaven on earth. We create healing for self and others. We are constantly in flux of choice: choosing to destroy or choosing to heal. We indulge in the pleasurable ways of knowing we are loving our selves and healing.

Coping with Physical Illness and Aging

The day before I faced an auditorium full of college students for a speaking engagement, I discovered spots on my face. I scrubbed, I searched mental knowledge … and then I remembered them as "age-spots" – something I'd read about and seen on others. On me? Vanity took over and my frightened ego rushed to a cosmetics counter later that afternoon. As I disclosed my horrible embarrassment of aging to the older woman behind the counter, she spoke to me of creams and covers and promises of fading and healing. And there was a moment, when her voice broke as she shared her own personal struggle with spots on her neck. We laughed as we momentarily connected as women facing horrible tragedy. When I left, I was changed. The spots no longer mattered because even the beautiful woman behind the expensive counter fought the same fight. I forget to use the creams, because they are no longer important to me. I lost the fear with the compassion of another woman who also faced. I let it go. I changed. I healed.

I have reason to focus on a state of healing. A few years ago I had a recurring dream. In the dream, which was always vivid, I was running in slow motion. The feeling evoked in the dream was one of utter fatigue because I was running so slowly and feeling such exhaustion and getting nowhere. I would awake from the dream feeling confused and disturbed because the dream was a metaphor for my life at that time. I'd been in the same teaching job for seventeen years and I was feeling powerless trying to keep up with increased pressure to perform and prove to the community and state my subject matter was worthwhile. Simultaneously, because of state decisions, I was cutting out the very beautiful creative units I most loved to teach – creative writing and a reader's workshop unit that promoted pure joy of reading. My deepest value in teaching is that all students need to be creative. Children in creative mode are seldom angry with selves and the world. I was stuck in a rational world of stress and expectation.

My own dear children had needs each night when I returned from work and somewhere in there I was a wife as well. I was sapped of energy. My health deteriorated and I developed unnerving symptoms. My stomach seemed to have shut down, my thinking became foggy, and about fifty percent of the time I felt feverish, though no fever would register. There were other symptoms as well, and they became increasingly bizarre. I wondered if I were dying.

In my depression, I began to believe the stories of never getting better and the mounting fatigue scared me. I was sleeping and missing my children's lives.

I kept thinking, "If only I weren't sick I could …" until one day I realized I possibly would not get better, but that I still needed to move on with life. Some inner reserve of the warrior segment of my spirit moved into my being. I forced myself to go running three times a week. I refused to live into the illness and continued to teach and speak – never missing a class during the three years of the disease. My arms became too weak to open some entrance doors to malls and stores, and so I began to do daily pushups. I knew my body was being poisoned, so I just kept drinking water and sweating – the only way I knew to detoxify.

My hope became other people: my spiritual director, my priest, my new coworkers at St. John's University, and Dr. Carol Ritberger. I now realize they taught me to *live out of my stories* and *into my potential.*

Carol taught me to stop compromising my integrity – a lesson I remind myself of daily. Carol is a miracle to all women she touches. She saw the toxins, she saw the emotional anguish, she saw my desire to be up in my head with God (seventh chakra). Her words were intimate and intense signs of healing and I recognized the truth of what she saw. I already knew on some level what she saw, but she named it all for me because I dared trust. I will spend the rest of my life savoring the angel she's been for me and for my family. Mostly, I knew she connected to me as a woman, a woman with a light of love to take to others. This book is sent with prayers and thoughts of my continued healing path of truth to give to anyone in need of a word, a phrase, a silence between phrases to speak what you presently need to hear.

I realized the more I let go of emotional distress, the more I grew intellectually, the more my physical health responded. I was saving myself when nobody else could. I threaded the thoughts of my intellect with the positive feelings of my emotions and created a veil of hope for my physical being. I listened, I noticed, I discerned, I prayed. And I magnificently became aware of healing. Years later, I would discover my running and pushups were the only things preventing a lapse into fibromyalgia.

Coping with Intellectual Thought

My intellect and will are imperfect. I suffer from food allergies and chemical sensitivities and I continue to make unhealthy choices that usually deter my healing. I cannot deny myself the very things I derive pleasure from: the occasional imported beer, the bruschetta, the pasta. I am in constant struggle with health and lack of health due to my decadent choices. Sometimes I choose poorly. The important piece is that most often I choose lovingly toward healing. We believe we have no choice, and we have so much limitless power with choice.This is what I *know*. We are predestined by genetics to certain weaknesses or predispositions to certain illnesses. Genetics cannot be changed and our realities are presented with difficulty. Just as we cannot change the images/stories we view in the media, we cannot change the images of the doctors who bring us the news we do not want to accept as new truth. And, yet, we are miraculously and powerfully in control of choice: of our decisions regarding attitude and our decisions about our physical health. Miracles occur all of the time. We exercise our right to choose hope rather than giving up. We allow intellect to have conscious thought of hope to take into our subconscious and unconscious levels. Soon the hope drifts into cellular level and flows through our bloodstream cleansing and healing and returning to pure form, familiar form of health. We choose to recognize miracles of healing.

Attitude toward intellect is power and control of spirit. We trust in the wholeness of intellectual thought connecting to emotions in a positive manner, just as Norm Cousins taught with his narrative of laughter therapy. Strengthening positive connection to emotions goes deeper into our very Selves to connect with inner spirit. Inner spirit heals and allows guidance to our wholeness, our life path, our life truth – our balance. We respond to language, only symbols in reality. Labels. We change our attitudes toward labels, toward wholeness of power amidst what we cannot change. We assume power of spirit relying on spiritual guidance to recognize our attitudes and our decisions.

Labels limit. Labels like "fibromyalgia" and "cancer" are devastatingly limiting as we move toward mind/body/spirit healing. We accept. We sort. We allow. We love all pieces and speak only lovingly moving into the trust of what is meant to be, but from a transcendent place of hope, happiness, and love for our body, mind, and spirit. Labels create rational and irrational fear beyond emotional readiness.. Labels take us where we do not want to go. We slowly interpret in the listening guidance of a larger truth. We look for understanding and resources to keep us in places of healing and hope and connection to Supreme Being. We create decisions made from the reality we create with limitless potential of wellness. Supreme Being knows mysteries we cannot.

Adam discovered his own imperfect intellect in the parable of the Garden of Eden. Intellect was darkened by will and Adam gave into to temptation rather than following divine truth. Adam was intimidated and feared. Adam made a mistake. The story exemplifies our universal weakness of intellect, and imperfection of following will rather than divine truth – usually out of intimidation or fear or temptation.

> ***Jesus calls us beyond this cultural hypnotic trance, beyond sleepwalking, by his countercultural actions. It's like the awakening clap of the Zen master's hand. He says we are trapped, we can't see. He tries by every means he can, often by way of parable, to subvert the normal way of seeing. Parables turn reality upside down.***
>
> – Fr. Richard Rohr

Cornstarch thickens the mango salsa I prepare as it gathers and binds the sweet of the mango and pineapple with the spice of the Asian chile paste and fish sauce. Intellect binds and thickens. It gathers the sweetness of emotion and self-love and blends with the spice and passion of our spirit to create the sustenance of wholeness. Broken spirits are gently mixed into wholeness and healing. Intellect is the cornerstone to our healing.

Intellectual thought births our emotional attitudes. Our bodies are formed toward healing or destruction as we send our messages. Physical form is a creation of intellect and cognitive knowing and sending of intellect to cellular, physical structure. A base of loving thought creates loving cells and being formed with emotions of hope, compassion, acceptance and love. *True form* remembered. Divine lenses of life experience bring us to remarkable paths and gestures of ultimate personhood, connection, and authority. *True form* is returning. Intellect is the precious cornerstone of all.

We remind our bodies we're okay. The other day I was feeling out of myself, a bit ill. I thought "You're okay" to my body – and I instantly felt effect. My body responded immediately by relaxing. *We're okay.* We create thoughts of gratitude.

Every moment we have breath is a moment of opportunity and gratitude. If we are alive today and breathing, we have potential, we have love, we have healing opportunity. Breathe into the next step of healing in gratitude and celebration of being alive. A student in my class delivers a speech valuing breath. She is from Africa and was almost hit by a city bus when she was five years old. She lives in gratitude from the experience of almost knowing death. She celebrates. True form created from gratitude in intellectual thought. Gratitude. Every day is gift. Every breath is gift. We remember.

"Pain is merely weakness leaving the body." The quotation is my intellectual mantra of positive narrative amidst aches and pains of temporary setbacks, womanhood, and effects of aging. In my intellectual imperfection I create a reality of health and limitless opportunity to savor life experiences of twilight skiing, delicious meals, and spiritual communion with the loving souls of my human experience.

Emotional Attitudes and Power of Choice

When our emotions are not okay, our bodies will let us know. First with a few aches and pains and later with devastating effects of stress and tension: diabetes, heart disease, and cancers threatening to eat away our beauty. We move into the rhythm of healing and recognize the serenity of wellness. Charles Swindall once said, "life is 10% what happens to us and 90% reaction." Reaction, coping, and spiritual guidance/connection are completely in our power. We intuit wellness, and the intuitive force defines the emotions of our divine truth and healing. True form of emotions is not created in the mind, it is created in the gut, in our intuition. Intuitively knowing is our power and we listen. I just began a yoga class and I was surprised to move into a state of ecstatic bliss at the end of the first session. I searched online and found an article from the "All Spirit Fitness" site that verbalized my ecstatic, profound experience. The "Corpse Pose" or "Shavasana" is intended for intuitive listening. According to the website, perfect Shavasana and Perfect Enlightenment are the same. I experience profound enlightenment of self-love and wholeness during Shavasana. Ironically, our very state of mindlessness brings us to mindfulness. The website states:

> ***Thought and intuition are two different things [that] the mind actually hampers intuition, and that intuition always has the right answer and mind rarely does. Shavasana is an opportunity for you to get in touch with that part of yourself that is 'no mind', the place where intuition lives.*** – www.allspiritfitness.com, *Shavasana101: What's So Hard About Playing Dead?*

Indeed, like the student who celebrates breath, it is our "death" which defines our life, our breath, our espiritu. Intuitive knowing is celebration and healing. We open our chakras and allow the light of our self-love and divine love to radiate from every pore and every opening, creating our wholeness and healing. Life is a process of dying to and healing.

Play and laughter are rememberances of fun and spirit. Our spirit knows play. It is celebration of emotion. Our bellies engage in full peels of laughter and we release, we let go of all toxic emotion. I laugh often. When I had dis-ease, the laughter was uneasy. I now laugh fully and completely when a friend and I wrestle for the check at a business lunch, or when my best friend and I write research and the, commas, are always, too frequent. I run from the hottub to create a snow angel in snow and my body stings with the shock of impulsive change in temperature. I play. I race a colleague to the xerox machine and shove him out of the way. Life is fun. Life is full of erotic, sensual pleasures to be savored and amusing moments of connectedness while sharing a same perception of fun. We share in our joy and ecstatic knowing with our chortles and chuckles and guffaws and shouts and tears of delight of play.

Ultimate Coping: Heartfelt Silence

Personal relationship with Supreme Being allows us to let go of despair and our feeble attempts to control life experience. Vivid images of experience of being fully present with Supreme Being are every bit as detailed in memory as the horrific images of John Lennon's death, and September 11, and vastly more meaningful in path toward healing. Graces, blessings and noticings of Supreme Being while communing balance human experience of violence and destruction. The matrix point of our balance is the vision of our healing into true form. We intuit wisdom in silence.

> ***Silence contains everything in itself. It is not waiting for anything; it is always wholly present in itself and it completely fills out the space in which it appears.***
>
> – Picard, *The World of Silence*,

Our culture has a negative perception of silence. Indeed, we talk too much and listen too little. Silence needn't be feared, silence is embraced as the loving aloneness experience of wellness and divine truth of acceptance. Silence is reflection and sacredness, but the created reality of our society teaches otherwise. When people are silent, we nonverbally interpret negativity. Private ephiphanies of love and healing occur in silence. Contemplative Listening allows love, compassion, and oneness to be received by heart and intuition. Communing with self is a healing experience of heart and head knowing … receiving and receiving and receiving lavishing energies of strength and power. Imperfect intellect listens to perfect intellect. Communing with perfect intellect blooms into loving experience, roses and kisses on the grey of our beings: "To love and be loved" (Phillipians 1: 3-8). Spiritual communion and loving bliss.

Our cognition is miraculously transformed. We empower healing when we name our fears, sort our fears, identify our needs and assert these needs in quality relationships and in relationship with Supreme Being. We let go of some fears. We listen in compassion and receive only love. We *know* love in our heart and our heads. We shape our thought and we shape our *true form*.

Fear prevents miracles – it constipates rather than allows the natural rhythm of letting go and releasing toxic energy. Bodies know healing, they need only recognize. I was full of fear in my dis-ease. Ultimate healing abides when wisdom replaces brokenness. Life is a mystery, but our reactions needn't be. My spiritual director has a candle of Hope she lights at the beginning of our sessions. Knowing I'm in a safe place to sort with someone who deeply knows unconditional love is everything I need. The candle of hope amidst my suffering brings me to tears every time. Tears are so healing – they literally remove toxins as they allow catharsis. Purity allows noticing of spirit. I used to joke about the Pavlovian effect the candle seemed to have on bringing me to immediate tears. Yet still, in my dark moments,

I envision the same candle of hope and I pray for the healing tears. Choosing reaction is choosing hope.

I met with my spiritual director. She heard a psychologist remark our Ego, which holds our fear (and holds up captive) is actually formed by age seven. I currently feel uncomfortable speaking in front of certain audiences, and we sorted in contemplative presence. I returned to my age seven and the experience of a first grade teacher who accused me of cheating. In truth, I was showing a friend we were almost done with a workbook rather than divulging correct answers. I was called in front of the class and repeatedly questioned, until I broke down and said what she wanted to hear, that I'd cheated. I denied my personal truth of innocence, simply to say what she apparently wanted to hear. My desk was moved into a corner for a full week, and then she called me in front of the class to ask if I were "good enough" to come back. I was ashamed and bad in that moment of judgment. Spiritual sorting allowed me to recognize I sometimes still feel like the girl in front of the class, full of fear I'm not "good enough". It's amazing the way we allow the stories of fear formed in our Ego to direct us as adults. Spiritual insight teaches us the path to our healing. We are no longer captive.

Healing: Creating New, Beautiful Stories.

Our Ego is constantly telling our hearts we are not safe, we need to worry. The state of the human experience is to be born into a life full of beauty – only to learn of eventual death. We spend our lives enjoying our moments of happiness and beauty while we wait for the other shoe to fall – the moments of pain, sorrow, and suffering. Ego creates false realities of protection by thinking ahead to potential states of fear or suffering. The mind fights to control. We remember the shavasana experiences and move into mindlessness and mindfulness. We fight the urge to create brain connectors with fear and negativity. Dr. T. Berry Brazelton warns that emotions are "internal architects, conductors, or organizers of our minds." True form exists in connectors of divine love.

Fears can spiral into addiction, further preventing healing internal architecture. Addictions prevent emotional coping. Behavioral therapists know the emotional development of the patient parallels the age the usage began. In other words, the adult may still be manifesting behaviors of coping similar to a much younger age child. Maturing in emotional coping brings confidence and strength to pursue and handle life experiences, including sickness, pain, and suffering. Emotional growth is prerequisite to healing. Repeated experiences of spiritual bliss and communion create magnificent internal architecture while illuminating a path that forms faith. Faith of knowing "*we're okay*". We remind our bodies at each level of healing.

Faith is only and, yet, miraculously (in truest sense), all we have. Faith and Hope distinguish us as those who don't give up amidst struggle because we *know* differently. I am in awe of souls able to move forward in strength and hope amidst human labels of sickness and deterioration. I am in awe of souls who heal, despite mere words. Our bodies and souls know what our minds cannot, and awareness is key to discovery.

Books of faith of all religions offer parables of hope, as do conversations in relationships placed gently before us at just the right time and in just the right place for us to recognize what we need for individual healing. We take it. We take our healing.

Mindfully present moments are healing. Each time we pray and/or meditate, we use our right-brain experience to create connection with rational left-brain. Rational connection with *beyond rational.* Strength of connectors grow: left and right brain; heartfelt experience of love and mindful experience of love; hope amidst hopelessness. Ultimate coping. We return, as when we were born, to pure, beautiful health of mind, body and spirit. Indeed, we return to *True Form.*

Somewhere between heaven and hell
A soul knows where it's been
I want to feel my spirit lifted up
And catch my breath again
Lay me down in the river
And wash this place away
Break me down like sand from a stone
Maybe I'lll be whole again one day.

– Crosby, Nash "Lay me Down", Sanctuary

Chapter Eleven

A Dance to the Rhythm of Forgiveness and Restored Peace

The feminine ways within men and women alike and within all life are the doorways to the beyond. For they are ways that listen, allow, and receive. And they know the unpredictibility of the forces of creation, know that the divine suddenly enters the celebration through new music, new dance steps. And if we are to join the party, if we allow ourselves to become, as the Sufis say, "drunk with the wine of the Beloved," we have to unburden ourselves from our outdated approaches to life, the divine, and even to love. – Hilary Hart, *The Unknown She*

Anger doesn't do any good. The words frightened me and I struggled to keep focusing on driving. Another coincidence … related to the book. At the time, I experienced a lining up of uncanny coincidences as I read a book about the visionaries who sighted Marian apparitions in Medjugorie, Bosnia. The voice stopped my entire being because I instantly knew the source experience, but I didn't know the reaction. Let me back up a bit. I read about Medjugorie to better understand a trip someone I knew was taking to receive healing for her child (the child remains healed ten years later). At this time of my life, I was much less in communion with my spiritual self, yet as I read the book, I was taken by how *it* seemed to know me so well it could actually respond to my critical reactions and unwillingness to believe. I read a chapter and then did load of laundry. As I moved, I questioned the "reality" of the spiritual experiences described in the book. The following chapter revealed exact replies to the very questions in my critical thought! A second time, I thought as I prepared cappucino, only to return again to immediate response to my critical questions in the very next pages I read. The third time it happened, I remember putting the book down on my lap and seriously wondering what was happening. Then there was the chapter of a rose, just as I received a single rose in my own human experience--serendipity. I took notice. The writer of the novel claimed Supreme Being spoke directly to him. This was too much for me to accept and I simply stopped reading – for awhile. How could a human interpret thoughts as rooted in Supreme Being? Wishful thinking, I thought … or craziness. Until the day my husband and I had a fight as I left to visit my grandmother in a town two hours away. We seldom left in anger, but I needed to keep schedule in order to return before dark. I left, and listened to music as I always did. Suddenly, a thought interrupted me so sharply – it cut off my own thought. **It interrupted**. It was not **my** thinking, yet it was in my cognitive awareness. *Anger doesn't do any good.* The phrase resonated strongly and I knew it was not my own. The emphasis was on the word "good" and I just didn't speak that way … my own phrasing/speaking natural pattern would have emphasized the word "anger". Later, when I returned to the book and reread, I learned the writer also experienced **completely interrupted thought**. Wow … what was this? Divine Intervention? Me? Doesn't Supreme Being speak to bible-bangers and people who fundamentally live scripture? I drink margaritas in the hottub – can't be me. I've been listening to that phrase ever since. Indeed, *Anger doesn't do any good.*

We can't eliminate anger, since it's a necessary reaction to injustice. In fact, it can be the very catalyst of our making change for the better. The problem comes when we remain in our anger, become stuck in our angry, victimized place.

> ***When a woman has trouble letting go of anger or rage, it's often because she's using rage to empower herself. While that may have been wisdom at the beginning, now she must be careful, for ongoing rage is a fire that burns her own primary energy ... the fieriness of rage is not to be mistaken as a substitute for a passionate life.***
>
> – Clarissa Pinkola Estes, *Women Who Run with the Wolves*

If we're to *do good* to ourselves and others, we need to first work through our anger by process of forgiveness. Forgiveness is a psychological and communicative construct. It's a process of healing. We move into forgiveness expecting to find healing for the other we're forgiving. Surprisingly, it is our own healing that occurs when we decide to move into forgiving process. We no longer carry the burden. We can't love and be loved when we're toxic with anger at each thought or appearance of another who's caused us harm. Our brains recognize visual stimuli connected to an anger response and repeatedly send this message out to the rest of the body, literally strengthening the synapses and patterns of destructive response. We cleanse destructive pattern every single time we send loving, forgiving messages as reaction to the same visual stimulus. Spiritual path even brings us to ecstatic knowing of divine love, but only through processes of forgiveness: first, in order to be reconciled with self and, second, to be reconciled with divine. We gently work to remove barriers of fear, addictions, unhealthy relationships, and expectations of Self and Ego, which also create barriers to forgiveness. Each time we sort and become fully present to what is needed in our relationships, we calmly see clarity in our true path of human experience. Calm abiding takes work. We become vulnerable. We open and discern relationship. We fight our urge to retaliate, and/or seek vengeance, which are counterintuitive to our healing.

Anger, hostility, and revenge are normal reactions to betrayal, pain, and manipulation. I walk the same world as you and I know well my mistakes and retaliations to those who've hurt me. I've made my mistakes and I work to accept them all – lovingly. I rid myself of shame. Elizabeth Super, licensed psychologist states, "Shame is a wasted emotion – it serves us no good in our culture." Indeed, we work to release our shame and our regret. We let go. We release. We cleanse. We focus our energy toward healing, rather than expending it and allowing it to dissipate in destructive pattern. Additionally, we unbury the hurt/anger we never retaliated and simply buried deep within. We deserve only love and life is a constant challenge to come back to a loving place. Anger continues to destroy intellectual, physical, emotional and spiritual self until new stories of forgiveness create love, vision, and clarity-- which is the healing process of letting go. My intent is to lovingly give you the experience and pieces of process.

Defining Forgiveness

A dictionary definition tells us to forgive is to pardon. Indeed, it is multi-faceted and potentially so much more. A process of forgiveness allows a return to love and healing and reconciliation with Supreme Being.

All relationships are a double-edged sword because of our need to be vulnerable in order to establish the quality relationships of trust. As such, we stand to be hurt,--dreadfully, at any given moment. Frank D. Fincham, a professor in the social and clinical psychology programs at SUNY and a former Rhodes scholar, states in his article "The Kiss of the Porcupines: From Attributing Responsibility to Forgiving.":

> ***Imagine how two porcupines huddled together in the cold of an Alaskan winter's night, each providing life-sustaining warmth to the other. As they draw ever closer together the painful prick from the other's quills leads***

> ***them to instinctively withdraw – until the need for warmth draws them together again. This "kiss of the porcupines" is an apt metaphor for the human condition, and it illustrates the two fundamental assumptions upon which this article is based: humans harm each other and humans are social animals. Acceptance of these two assumptions results in challenge addressed in this article – how to maintain relatedness with fellow humans in the face of being harmed by them.***

Indeed, it is precisely the relationships that bring us our joy, our connectedness to others, our inspiration, and our passion which also stand to tear our hearts right out of our chests. We wonder how to move on. We live in dismay others can survive without us while we feel as if we've lost our left arm. We literally feel less than whole. We examine and sort as we notice Supreme Being intent for our relationships with self and others. Carolyn Myss's book *Sacred Contracts* describes divine intent for placing people in our lives at just the right time, in just the right place. We are then in contract with the person until divine intent is completed. Some people are angels guiding us to truth and shining only in loving relationship. Others are life lessons taught through pain of betrayal and struggle. Our most painful experiences teach us the most valuable lessons – if we allow the healing process of letting go and seeing what we are meant to know. I'm currently in pain as I move through a process of letting go of a dear friend. To choose to remain in pain sends repeated signals from the heart to the head of the pain – and the pain moves into our cognitive synapses and connectors and moves through our body into our cellular structure. We literally destroy our physicality when we remain in pain instead of healing. The trust and betrayal cycle of human imperfection reminds us of our right to be loved as we deserve. A struggle back to wholeness regains the use of the left arm. *Forgiveness Births Wholeness.*

Acknowledging the pain is the first step. Burying still sends destructive messages to mind and body. Even in quality, loving relationship, there is imperfection and pain. As Fincham says, "imperfection of any partner means that hurt or injury is inevitable, but more poignant precisely because we have made ourselves vulnerable" (p. 2). Human condition is imperfect, thus allowing all to suffer the consequences of the other's imperfection. We also create suffering through our own err. Indeed, to err is human, to forgive divine. Contemplative listening of silence weighs the consequences of choice. When Burt Reynolds left Loni Anderson, the media reported that Loni refused to live in anger and "create facelines" of anger. Her lighthearted response also holds a deep truth. Pausing to notice faces of others reveals the wrinkles of pain and anger left unresolved. Life seems a struggle and the competitiveness and hurt create contours in once peaceful faces. The challenge is to remain loving amidst the pain of relational conflict or closure. What do our faces convey? Love and ability to try again? To trust? What do we tell the very cells of our body to create as image to others? Healing is a process of justice, acceptance and forgiveness.

Psychologically, we need the framework of forgiveness in order to re-establish a relationship. Even more necessary for any relationship to genuinely survive, is a need to establish the supportiveness and trust previously established. A wrong causes individuals in relationship to choose to end or to continue. Continuing relationship deserves a construct to re-establish the goodwill and intent between two individuals. Fincham also is clear about necessary components leading to need of forgiveness. Injuries that are purely unforeseen and unintentional do not need forgiveness. There is nothing to forgive. Also, "forgiveness occurs in full knowledge that the transgressor is responsible for the injury, that he or she thereby forfeits any right to the victim's sympathy, affection or trust, and that the victim has a right to feel resentful" (p. 4). The significance of responsibility is necessary. Resentment without named or sorted responsibility and/or intent from another being is simply wasted energy. Particularly in romantic relationships, the very act of falling in love creates a false image of the other. We fail to recognize the very faults creating the mistakes of the future – and they reciprocate this clouded view. Sometimes women even acknowledge certain weaknesses as the relationship continues, but mistakenly believe the other will change – will quit getting drunk so often once there are children, will quit looking at others with romantic interest, and the list goes on. Indeed, we struggle to find the line that allows us to love unconditionally, yet see the other in his/her truth and imperfection.

I've been married for almost twenty years. My husband has learned to put up with my imperfections: my underwear left strewn on the bathroom floor or my idiotic manner of washing dishes with the suds in the "wrong" side of the kitchen sink. Further, I have a desire to always look for opportunity, growth, and change while he is content and satisfied exactly where we are in life path. Just as I learn to accept qualities in his behavior, he accepts mine. This acceptance of behaviors does not necessitate need for forgiveness, merely a "putting up with" as relationship continues. Fincham is distinct between the notion of condoning and the need of forgiveness. He states, "the partner's commitment to behavioral change, either explicitly or implicitly through apology, facilitates forgiveness. In contrast, acceptance implies that "change on the part of the perpetrator is no longer necessary" (Christensen, Jacobson, & Babcock, as cited in Fincham, 2000). Perhaps we reconcile ourselves to a situation, and view it anew.

Forgiveness is deeper. Forgiveness is a promise to change. Forgiveness begins with an apology, genuine remorse, and desire to change or intend to not repeat the previous hurtful action. It's possible to apologize without the aforementioned components, but why would a person with self-love accept less? The intent to change is a promise. Time is a necessary component to rebuilding the trust and to following through with change. A person who is unfaithful to a co-worker's intimate conversation, a romantic partner who shares intimacy with another, a friend who betrays all have a second chance to show loving affirmation in relationship. Certainly, failure to do so brings another level of distrust due to established history. A repeated mistake in future now creates a pattern of unwillingness to change and to repeat the hurt. We trust our connection with self to name, to sort, to discern the closure in relationship or desire to remain vulnerable and risk future pain. In the end, we weigh the pros and cons of qualities and behaviors in the other. We choose accordingly, but we always choose from a place of self-love – not self-abuse.

Relationships that survive the apology and follow-through the changed behavior re-establish trust, and provide a history of caring and intent to respect the relationship in future conflict or hurt. I recently had to apologize for a behavior toward my best friend. I had a summer of difficulty and change and saw no reason to keep boxes of files related to our research, especially when I hadn't heard from her in quite some time, and I was in pain because I misinterpreted her busyness as our friendship de-escalating in intimacy. I threw away the boxes in order to release the pain, and the confusion. My heart ached and my gut reacted each time I thought of her and missed her. Fortunately, I realized later we were still very dear friends. I had to confess what I'd done with the boxes – and I was simultaneously embarrassed, frightened, and reminded of the earlier pain. I still remember my heart and my gut experiencing the previous anguish as I spoke to her of my error. Do you know how it felt to receive compassion and forgiveness and restore a precious friendship? Now I am even able to laugh – and we do. We are best friends who shop, who have lunch, who laugh and love each other and that is gift. We are fortunate in our forgiven relationships. Forgiveness is gift.

When we are wronged, it's natural to want retribution, vengeance, ill will toward the other. In fact Smedes lists three stages of "unfair pain" (p. 58): 1) the original wallop, 2) remembering the wrong that happened, and 3) the vengeance stage, "the futility of wishing at least equal pain on the person who gave her pain. If the victim allows herself to get mired in the third stage, she will allow the person who hurt her once to go on abusing her in her memory until she dies." See, this is the thing – we forgive to move on and heal and move into our loving, limitless potential in life and regain deserved happiness. The catalyst of change is our emotional reaction to the very stimuli that once brought reactions of anger and pain. Our emotional reactions of love heal us every time we experience the other in heartfelt knowing and cleansing. We become changed. We become healed.

Otherwise we continue to punish ourselves, sabotage ourselves and create our own limits and victimization. We exercise choice to stop being hard on ourselves and move into gentleness. We choose to accept or move into process of change through the cleansing of self-forgiveness. Self-forgiveness is dualistic in a process of contemplative listening. Divine experience provides loving view of the error or imperfection of our experience. Relationship of transcendent spirit with human experience is the necessary psychological construct to 1) name the person responsible and own the pain, 2) state apology, and 3) move into promise to change. Silence births the purity of forgiveness in a state of contemplative listening. We love the little girls who felt "bad", and the college age women who took risks and dared to grow and have fun and experience – sometimes acting against inner truth and wisdom in the very act of growing and maturing. We pick them up in the arms of our transcendent hearts and we love them as we would any other deserving child or young woman. We forgive any past experiences that bring us any regret or remorse. The combination brings a lens of viewing self and world with a richer, stronger countenance. We walk the walk of our human experience knowing we accept ourselves, knowing we forgive ourselves, and knowing our unconditional love of self. Again, we are fortunate. Lou Smedes, author of *Forgiving Ourselves* explains the authentic reason to forgive self.

> ***We feel a need to forgive ourselves because the part of us that gets blamed feels split off from the part that does***

the blaming. One self feels despised and rejected by the other. We are exiled from our own selves, which is no way to live. This is why we need to forgive ourselves and why it makes sense to do it: We are ripped apart inside, and forgiving ourselves is the only way we heal the split.

We forgive ourselves and other as a means to healing. Those who ruminate rather than forgive self need extra focus and love for healing. Fincham states the following descriptors of forgiveness:

Forgiving is intentional.
Forgiving is unconditional.
Forgiveness is a gift. It's altruistic.
Forgiveness is distinct from reconciliation and reunion.
– Frank Fincham, "The Kiss of the Porcupines", *Personal Relationships*

It's quite possible to reunite with someone without forgiving him/her. I know many couples who remain married for children, financial need, or fear of being alone. They reunite, but may not forgive. Reconciliation includes forgiveness, but forgiveness does not necessarily lead to reconciliation. A close friend hurt me a few years back. We met for coffee and discussed the situation in a high-backed oak booth that cloaked our words and tears of honesty from others. It turns out I'd hurt her as well. It's amazing how we focus on our experience, often neglecting feelings of the other, or vice versa. Both perspectives are necessary. We talked, we cried some more. In the end, we didn't reconcile our friendship, but we transcended the need to be awkward around each other when our paths crossed. We forgave and moved into spiritual love. When we see each other, even now, years later, we hug. We love each other. There is no pain, only forgiveness. Forgiveness is gift. The epiphany and process of forgiveness make us whole again.

"I'm so sorry I hurt you," are words that promise. Forgiveness is a process over time after an initial step of remorse. The first step is the apology, but time heals or teaches the necessary lesson in each particular sacred contract with others. The virtue of patience reveals what is lovingly meant to be. Some relationships end, some reconcile, and many bring gifts of forgiveness and truth. Reconciliation is a byproduct, a promise in future that may or may not occur.

Justice

Anita Hill so aptly illustrated legal system's ability to care for those in submissive imbalance of power. When betrayal is caused by the very ones we look to for protection and safety, in the workplace, and in places of healing through counseling and medical assistance, we can choose to retaliate with legal action. Justice allows us to retaliate in an ethical manner. Choice is power. However; it bears noting that many who choose to retaliate are simply remaining in the anger, rather than moving into process of healing. Lawsuits, for example, can be very lengthy processes. There are important questions to ask one's self when choosing appropriate steps of healing. First, will the legal action prevent others from being harmed? It is our obligation to prevent harm for others. Second, what are the true damages to personhood? Many times, our courts are clogged with the fluff cases created by those who are simply looking for attention, looking to sabotage further success and live as victim, or looking to retaliate from places of competitiveness or power, rather than ethical change for good. Living in the energy of victimization stifles healing when there is a means of forgiveness process to move forward into healing. Finally, is the legal action keeping the pain or allowing a letting go and/or healing of pain? Assessing true damages allows contemplative discernment to honor personhood and make decisions about self-love and healing.

Justice and forgiveness are the only ways to move on out of pain. Smedes writes the story of Susan Struthers who came home and discovered the mutilated bodies of her parents after Charles Manson and others had gruesomely murdered in a drug-induced state. Susan suffered a nervous breakdown, and when she recovered she also became aware of spiritual healing. At the same time, Charles Watson, one of the brutal murderers was serving time and also found awareness of spiritual experience. Susan learned of his conversion and drove to see him. As Smedes so eloquently states, "she stopped looking for meaning in the past and did what she had to do to find meaning in her future. She held out her hand to Watson and said the impossible words: I forgive you" (p. 34). Although she tried to testify for a lighter sentence for Watson, she used the experience to begin a promise to move on … into healing and becoming.

Lisa Barnes Lampman, editor of *God and the Victim* explains that while forgiveness occurs, justice remains a constant. Justice is consequence of a hurtful act and, as such, is separate from compassion and loving acts of forgiveness and acceptance. Someone who has done someone a wrong in a criminal manner follows the same construct of forgiveness and the same need for contemplative listening and discernment. She states:

> ***Discerning whether true repentance has taken place, particularly with an offender who has committed violent acts, requires prayer, discernment, and wise counsel from others who have intimate knowledge of the offender's attitude and behavior. Forgiveness of the offending act does not relieve the offender from consequences, nor does it necessitate a re-establishment of trust on the part of the victim.***

My perception is to discern what's best to allow the moving on, rather than inertia. Letting go can come from legal action, and letting go can also come from ritualistic personal closure. When I leave a position of employment, I lovingly say goodbye to each room and its memories. When I leave a person, I lovingly ritualize the closure in the appropriate means for the individual. I send them off with blessing and love – even as I am hurting. Rituals are justice. Whether literal or figurative, justice is gift of choice.

Acceptance

The Dalai Lama and Thich Na Hanh teach transcendence of oneness with Supreme Being. The nature of meditative perceptions of all principles in Eastern religion focuses on letting go of human experience and moving into oneness with divine. The process eliminates a need for forgiveness, which is dualistic relationship. Acceptance of all that is with intent to live within the principles of divine achieves true path. Thus, the individual accepts flaws and wrongs of human experience with lens of knowing love and intent not to repeat the wrong. Acceptance brings the dividedness or confusing opposites of the soul back into wholeness and becomes one. The soul becomes healed as it moves into transcendent stages of oneness.

Forgiveness and Religious Perspective

Stating remorse for an act, followed by a statement of intent to forgive is not complete forgiveness accomplished. A statement of intent to forgive begins a process, which over time, proves to move toward or away from the truth of a relationship. Time heals the wounds as forgiveness fills in the holes of destruction and pain with love. Fincham cites the research of Thoresen, Luskin, and Harris (1998, p. 164) to illustrate global understanding of forgiveness. "Certainly it appears that forgiveness is a "goal commonly advocated by all of the world's longstanding religions."

A Jewish perspective of forgiveness is explained in the article "ELLUL: A Time to Reflect" which is based on a class by Rabbi Yaacov Haber. Jewish perspective finds three levels of forgiveness: "Selichah", "Mechilah", and "Kapparah".

"Selichah" represents the first step of intent to be forgiven by either man or divine. The statement "I am sorry for what I did; I sincerely regret having done it, and I will never do it again (1)" includes all the necessary components of a message or request for the process of forgiveness. Psychologically, everything is included to save face of the injured party. Remorse equalizes the relationship after a weight of pain and injury has left one party holding more vulnerability. Remorse is a return to vulnerability and balance. A promise never to do it again renews intent to re-establish current trust. Jewish faith acknowledges any refusal to be cruel. Appropriate response is forgiveness process.

"Mechilah" is usually translated as "wiping away" (1). The required response is to attempt to re-establish the relationship as it was before the transgression. A woman searches her heart to mindfully discern appropriate response, and with the power of her God as support moves into an opening up and allowing trust to return. A "wiping away" signifies the relationship begins anew and past transgressions are not brought up again when conflict occurs.

"Kapparah" is a celebration of atonement, which usually is accomplished on Yom Kippurim. The statement "My conscience will not let me live with myself, because of what I did to you and to our relationship" searches a response which is transcendant and beyond human capacity (1). Power of divine intercedes to reconnect human with human and humans with divine. Day of Atonement on the tenth day after Rosh Hashana (57) reveals grace and blessedness and healing through forgiveness for all. Indeed, belief systems have process for moving into the process of forgiveness.

According to the *Catholic Encyclopedia*, Christians follow the teachings of 2 Corinthians 5:18 and look for "remission of sins, reconciliation with God, the graces of salvation and justification" (p. 57). The gift of Christ to suffer for human weakness and become divine in order to pardon weakness is the cornerstone of the faith of Trinity. Clarity comes when all obstacles between Jesus and individual are removed so forgiveness and unconditional love are reaffirmed in process of healing. Sometimes, the obstacle can even be man-made decisions as law of religion, which is discussed further in the next chapter. We remove all barriers and resume intimate relationship and we choose our healing – every time. We allow opportunity for forgiveness and healing. We allow all individuals to move into love they deserve – especially communing with Jesus, Holy Spirit, and God. We follow Christ's example to forgive seventy times seven, as many times as necessary. It's all healing and returning to love, in process.

Muslims reverently search for forgiveness and cleansing through pilgrimages to Mecca. One of the Five Pillars of Islam is to go on Hajj (the pilgrimage) once in an individual's lifetime. A website on religious tolerance explains:

> ***The Hajj consists of several ceremonies, meant to symbolize the essential concepts of the Islamic faith, and to commemorate the trials of prophet Abraham and his family. … Prophet Muhammad had said that a person who performs Hajj properly 'will return as a newly born baby [free of all sins]'. The pilgrimage also enables Muslims from all around the world, of different colors, languages, races, and ethnicities, to come together in a spirit of universal brotherhood and sisterhood to worship the One God together.*** (religioustolerance.org).

Dualistic religions like Christianity and Judaism necessitate a concept of forgiveness for true path. Initially, the "sin" is acknowledged through the lens of attrition and contrition. Attrition acknowledges human experience of desire, temptation, and sinfulness. Individuals seek the grace of God (and relief from the fear of hell) through Attrition. Indeed, attrition is grace. Further, contrition or sorrow moving to resolve weakness or sin because of remorse, and offense of God, in the sense of personal loving relationship brings deeper knowing of loving forgiveness.

Forgiveness and Healing

I wonder what the brain looks like in a state of healing and forgiveness. I imagine pink, healthy cells creating the passionate pulsating connectors of reaction to visual or sensual stimuli to grand emotions of love, forgiveness, and purest bliss of *knowing*. Tim McNamara, Reiki Master, touches the tips of his fingers together and separates his energy from the negativity of others as he repeats a mantra of "bless her, bless her, bless her". He instantly moves into loving reaction to toxic experience. I forgave the medication I used to take which brought me side effects of discomfort and moved into loving relationship, taking each pill with a prayer of healing. I no longer require the medication. Love and forgiveness heal. Hearts are full of light and contain no dark spots of hatred. Love is being poured into the holes in the heart created by the shard of glass which cut us wide open with experiences of less than loving. We allow the love to pour into our hearts and pulse throughout the being we are magnificently *becoming* until the pulsing of head and heart beat to a rhythm of our own *created healing*. Cleansing and clarity birth our limitless potential and deepest yearnings to be who we are meant to be in this world.

Return to wholeness is the result of determining individual path to healing and forgiveness, whether through psychological construct, or structure of religious establishment. Healing is a return to love, and women are the healing energy needed for each other and for the world. Without forgiveness, we continue into dis-ease through lost sense of love: for self, others, and divine relationship. Indeed, the obstacle of unnamed, unsorted, unacknowledged sin or wrong creates distance. Unconditional transcendent love is grace and blessing and/or oneness which satisfies our deepest longing and brings sense of harmony with all of nature. Unconditional love brings us to mindful discernment in our human relationships. We end the unhealthy, we nurture the healthy through a constant reciprocation of forgiveness and return to trust, love, and commitment to the work of the relationship – even amidst pain of imperfection. The candid work of sorting and remaining authentic humbly prepares us for the surprises and bliss of moving forward to the next luminary of our spiritual path in relationship with Supreme Being: walking a mandorla while being loved deeply and richly. We create a clean heart. Our imperfections are "wiped away" by a God who doesn't even remember them and we are cleansed and made pure, as children. We move forward from an ultimate space of love and opportunity to love. Forgiveness is necessary healing and wholeness.

Seventy times seven. The Bible teaches Christians to forgive as many times as necessary. We discern our spiritual path and move into acceptance and forgiveness. We are called to move forward and transform ourselves anew. Life situations and pain provide opportunity for us to notice epiphanies and grandeur of human and divine acceptance, reconciliation, and forgiveness. We move from the conventional stage of contrition and into the belongingness and owning of attrition with personal knowledge of Supreme Being and response. *Anger does no good.* The words no longer frighten me as they did while I drove. They now fill me with love and tenderness as I continue to ponder the many layers of meaning the phrase has in my experience. *Anger does no good.* **We** do. We do good. We become clean. We *do good.*

Without forgiveness there is no future.

– Archbishop Desmond Tutu (1998)

The real miracle is not to walk either on water or in thin air, but to walk on earth – Thich Nhat Hanh

Chapter Twelve

Embracing the Mystical

I feel somehow strangely compelled
Under moonlight I stood wild and naked
Felt no shame just my spirit awakened.
– Neil Finn, "Sinner"

Secret fun. Anyone who has ever skinnydipped knows the pleasure of gliding through water effortlessly. Moonbeams mirrored on wavetops reflect luminous moments of tranquility and laughter with others. The coolness and secret thrill of stolen nakedness and freedom rebels against constraints of clothing and society simultaneously. Body awakens. Being naked is an experience of vulnerability that evolves into an experience of interior and exterior freedom. No wonder this is such a prevalent theme for some women at college. As we figuratively learn how to express ourselves come into being, the metaphor of revealing physical self extends the vulnerability and openness necessary for learning and seeing life from new lens. Nakedness is a means of becoming vulnerable and, yet, sensing "okayness." Nakedness brings us into our created beauty and opens us to opportunity. We learn trust each and every time. When we dare to express ourselves through our Creative Self, we experience a sense of vulnerability and nakedness. The opportunity of these moments creates our growing edges because we sense our constancy and power in the decisions we arrive at through spiritual discernment. We are fully aware of our inner power. Created works of art are attempts to touch others with magnificent truths and beauty, but can only be done through daring to reveal naked truths. We glimpse experiences transforming our created being into beyond rational knowing as we intuit our limitless potential.

Being on a stage taught me to comfortably be in front of others. Assuming a character allowed me to be vulnerable to others as someone else as I eased into the comfort of my own skin. Psychological comfort was derived from being anyone but myself and receiving applause at the end of a show. The chemistry of working with others and cast parties at 417 Hamilton House are some of my most cherished memories. However, my participation in Forensics (speech team) held even more meaning for my growth into authenticity. On an almost weekly basis, I learned to express myself to audiences and others performing **my** individual interpretation of phenomenal literature, or **my** ideas in organized format. These, too, received applause and acceptance. I competed at the National level. While celebrating with teammates I was bonded to them more intimately than I've ever experienced – and I still know some of them twenty years later. I was accepted in my truth. Further, I belonged as I voiced my truth. We played and created such fun memories of staying in hotels, dancing each evening, meeting others, laying out in the Kentucky sun, and performing excellence. The dynamics of theatre and forensics are where I most came into myself: a process of moving from validation of applause to knowing my own affirmation. I remember late night discussions challenging establishments and we found our deepest values as we discovered philosophy and insight … noticing the "ahas".

My friend, Andrew, taught me the most valuable lesson: to view life situations as more than just black and white, to look beyond and think outside the box. There is always new information, something else we haven't seen yet. Our search for the new information we've not yet discovered is adventure of life. This book focuses on the conflict of living: internal and external dissonances that are constantly sorted within a divine context of discovering the "aha" or new information, or epiphany of truth. We express ourselves from the embrace of our experiences: our deepest power of knowing and we continue to look for new information in gray areas extending us beyond limitations and into creative response. Our constancy in an unsure life experience is derived from the confidence of knowing and connecting our spiritual truths.

I see profound connection with Neil Finn's lyrics at the start of the chapter, since they provide a vivid image of experiential truth. We allow vulnerability and nakedness to lead us. It is in our nakedness that we experience openness and trust and faith. He asks the profound question, "Where's my faith, is it lost?" More importantly, he voices the response, "Can't see it till I cast it off." We spend our whole lives desiring to own, embrace, unconditionally live and love our faith, our trust, our life creed. We own it because we cast it off in order to sort, to see, to find the new information we need to own it. When we own our creed for life, and our experience of taking that out to others, we stop desperately grasping, clamoring for something to believe in. We are no longer out of sorts, we are certain. We mystically arrive at our intended being, truth, power of existence. Joy prevails from this place of knowing. Secret fun of dancing through life.

Living life with the brakes on is just no fun. We remove boundaries of limitation and see the magnificence of our created inner child playing through life in gifted form. Created Beings fully embrace life meaning and know happiness. Decisions made in a spiritual manner never bring feelings of regret or remorse, only a sense of peace. Just as we free our bodies, we free our souls – interior and exterior freedom. Spiritual awakenings occur in the moments we are stripped bare of all constraints of human-made establishment – even religious establishments. We constantly flow in a rhythm of movement toward and away our definition of divine and our definition of community expression of unconditional love and Higher Good.

The rhythm of embracing religious expression comes only in the mysticism of experiential knowing. My friend, Zane, went whale-watching at a time when whales had not been sighted for two months. Yet they appeared. He and his wife experienced whales coming so magically close, they actually swam under the boat and seemed to play – a spiritual encounter to be sure. As Zane recounts the story, he knows the spirituality of the moment and I see it reflected in his eyes – intense seriousness. I believe his truth in that experience, the beauty of a moment when human spirit intuitively connected with whales at play who would approach with no fear and even roll on backs as if waiting for tummies to be rubbed in play. These are the moments we live for, the moments that are sure and true and that maintain us throughout life. We choose to adorn ourselves in a journey of choosing or noticing pieces that convey spiritual truths we wish to express to others.

I chose to adorn my spirit with the community of Catholicism after searching, owning, experiencing and noticing each sacred portion over a long period of time. I no longer listen to fear-based view in society toward mysticism. It is our mystical, ecstatic experiences that voice our deepest truth. Spiritual and mystical experiences of divine should be savored, not feared. I was brought to Catholicism through a connection of mystical knowing. Transubstantiation is a Catholic sacrament of believing bread is converted to the body of Christ and wine is converted to the blood of Christ at Eucharist. My rational thinking limited my acceptance and I struggled to understand. One Sunday, as my priest prayed this text of the liturgy, I was struck with such a moment of clarity. White light surrounded him and I became fully aware of his words, "This is the body of Christ. This is the blood of Christ." And suddenly, I knew in my heart and spirit it was true. He spoke the same words each Sunday for years, but in that moment of mystical knowing, I could fully accept transubstantiation. I adorn myself with the truth of my decision.

Another example of mystical truth occurred when my own spiritual director and I spoke as I discerned the final stages of moving into a vocation of spiritual direction. Again, I saw loving, luminescent holiness and light surrounding her. My memory is of her face and words becoming so brilliantly holy and luminous I could not even speak for a moment. Another moment of clarity because I saw differently. Admittedly, I struggled with such profound, divine message … as if it were even too much. Years later, I see differently … as I savor the experience. I was blessed with such profound mystical occurrences twice in my life, giving a precious certainty for both decisions: to be Catholic; to be a spiritual director. I know the extension of my gift to preciously own Catholic perspective as the root of my ability to openly do work with non-denominational, unconditional acceptance of all spiritual journeys. There is no doubt of my loving embrace of both. In life, suffering and self-doubt flow in and out of our lives and there is very little we can truly be sure about – but our spiritual experiences are our very confidence, security, and strength. Money, relationships, and health all ebb and flow as they come in and out of our lives … in fact, it is only our mystical spiritual occurrences that remain constant. The constancy of spirit is our wisdom and truth of being.

Wisdom brings us into relationship with others, with or without a religious community to exactly the truthful place of our intended being. It is this very magnificent countenance that is our rock of faith as we walk this world that calls our deepest values into question. We heal and we heal others from mystical places of belief that cannot be touched. We live the joy and fun of our loving, compassionate, and pure Being. We look to the moonbeams on wavetops to guide the way of our nakedness and become extended visions of interconnectedness.

Even if we erased all teachings of religious establishments or sacred text, we would still know personal relationship with divine: what Merton refers to as everything we need. When we find the loving support and compassion we experience in community with others who share our spiritual lens, it is rich and meaningful, in choirs and symphonies of interconnectedness. We choose wisely as we extend ourselves to others in community, so that we may fully embrace belonging. I belong to a religion that communes with my spirit – and I see authentic place among men and women in timeless connection. Communing with women: the mystic spirits of Julian of Norwich, and Gertrude of Helfta and Catherine of Sienna; Mary, mother of Jesus; and the nuns, spiritual directors and pastoral staff led me to such exquisite gentle knowing of my own power. I fully embrace the words of my priest as they lead me to Trinitarian relationship, connecting me further to spirit within. The Holy Spirit lives in my spiritual work and Christ lives in the experiences of my suffering and resurrection. God watches and waits and rejoices in my epiphanies of knowing. I know truth of my experiences through a lens of noticing, just as you will assuredly come to the exact place you are meant to be in your knowing. We embrace religious choice knowing religions are man-made, and thus imperfect, so we may experience loving community with others in spirit as we continue to do the work of the religious community and it's transformation over time.

There is astounding increase in awareness and integration of New Age thought in recent years. The New Age movement has grown for a variety of reasons: the millenium; misplaced feelings of those who are lonely or products of abusive upbringings; those who experience mid-life crisis; and those who've left religious communities in anger. Further, we all sense the ever-growing need to belong and feel control in a world with increasing fear and realities of terrorism and nuclear threat. The attraction of diverse, New Age thought is very much a part of our world. We need to see with lenses of spiritual truth: some New Age is preciously meaningful, some is fluff, and some is even dangerous. Enhanced learning comes from mindful choices as we listen to others who use crystals, connect with animal spirits, and read channeled books of spirit. We listen behind the experiences to discern depths of truth from shallow attempts to draw us in with misplaced desire for monetary success or desire to control.

I view all extensions of spirituality with a lens of twofold caution: does the "community" of belief address others, or is it based in ego? Can it be tied to a sacred text or base? Profound wisdom of discernment with contemplative self brings us to know the difference. It's like my experience of the Minneapolis Uptown Art Festival and later festivities, years ago. I remember dancing with my college roommate in afternoon sun of the reggae band, Shangoya, surrounded by booths of opals, pottery and artwork. The fun continued into the evening and many of us drove to a party in St. Paul. We mingled as we listened to Pink Floyd, Rolling Stones and filled cups of frothy, keg beer. While we enjoyed living in the fun of the moment, we saw others choosing a different reality--they were stoned. They spoke to no one, they never moved, they simply sat "in their own Private Idaho" as we used to say. The buzz from their pot most certainly provided an escape, a numbness, but they totally missed the reality of the party and the memories of fun shared by everyone else there. Was that their **intent**?

People behave similarly with spirituality. They look for the "buzz" or escape it provides, but forget to use it as lens with which to view reality and move into truth of place in the world. The complacency of this particular view of spirituality lies in its temporary "fix" or moment of bliss; it lacks transformation. Spiritual truth is active, not passive. Further, for many, these experiences remain in Ego rather than heart. For example, I hear women comparing the "best" yoga classes to take, people enrolling in meditation competing for the "best" experience of meditation, and churches providing the most "popular" place to be spiritual. Indeed, people even measure their spirituality in human terms. Studying spiritual books, enrolling in classes, and competing to meditate deeper will provide steps of reflection and prepare us for contemplation, but the **intent is always**

growth and transformation, in order to take spirit to others. We continue to live in this world and discern. We are not monopolized by a materialistic society of Ego because we are holding the "get out of jail free" card the entire time. Heartfelt experience is catalyst for mindful presence and knowing our place to change and affect our world. The abundance of living and acting accordingly moves us into the power of ultimate experience. Our truth is a life of living differently, abundantly, miraculously. We recapture the dream of being created for *intent*. Women, we are called to get up off the couch and join the party.

Mindful discernment also gives vision to see Truth of intent in religious communities, defined by base as tied to sacred roots and text. I was shocked to read a few years ago about the prevalence of cults in our culture:

> ***The cult problem is so prevalent, the chances of a family member joining a cult are greater than a family member catching chicken pox, four times greater than contracting AIDS, 90 times greater than contracting measles, and 45,000 times greater than contracting polio. We frequently see a great deal about bult tragedies in our media: Jonestown, Waco, Heaven's Gate – but the facts regarding cults are rarely divulged to the general public***
>
> – www.factnet.org, "Danger of Cults is Growing"

All diverse religious choices, as healthy communities of spirit, have stood the test of time and are built from sacred text. I once searched a questionable religion and discovered a leader who centered the membership upon himself. Cult leaders keep the focus of love, devotion, and allegiance on themselves. Ironically, very much in state of Ego. Authentic faith-based religious communities focus on God, Buddha, and Allah. Discernment is lifelong. Protect your spirit and the spirit of those around you – it's as easy as a quick search online, or a question to someone you trust to know. The consequences of unhealthy religion are devastating to mind/body/soul.

Gently Guiding Spirit to Others

We breathe the rhythm of life.

> ***Woman is more filled than man to make exploration and take bolder action in nonviolence ... there is no occasion for women to consider themselves subordinate or inferior to man. ... Woman is the companion of man, gifted with equal mental capacity. ... If by strength is meant moral power, then woman is immeasurably man's superior. ... If nonviolence is the law of our being, the future is with women.*** – Ghandi

Authentic, spiritual relationship guides us to our feminine style of connectedness and becomes the masculine style of our power and action. Sophia God is feminine and connected, as lights illuminating night sky, rather than masculine style of hierarchy. Women nurture interconnected relationships taking spirit to others, in wholeness. *We have already been given everything we need to do so.*

I am interconnected with the truth of Gertrud of Helfta, a mystic from the 1200's. She saw clarity and provided writings of a description of friendship and intimacy with God based on faith as relationship (Klimisch as cited in *Medieval Woman Monastics*). Gertrude wrote of her "heart knowledge" of God's return to us in our earliest biblical tradition of the heart as organ of knowing. The passion within is born in personal relationship with our image of divine and feminine spirit: Sophia God lives in connectedness and in the organs of our hearts and knowing as we notice mystical truth. Sophia God connects me to Gertrud and to modern day mystics, like Sobonfu Somé, a contemporary mystic in San Francisco. I see vivid expression of my truth in her words as she explains why we walk among others, rather than in isolation as spiritual beings:

> ***a sense of disconnection and isolation is damaging to feminine energy because isolation is counter to the nature of feminine spirit, which is about relationship and wholeness. It is the turning against its own nature that is the real source of vulnerability in feminine spirit. 'The only thing that can disempower feminine spirit is feminine power turning back on itself,' she says."*** – *The Unknown She*

We See our Image of Divine in Others.

My husband and I visited Louisville, just a brief drive from the monastery where Thomas Merton, a spiritual mentor, once wrote. He isolated himself to write at Gethsemane monastery, but richly brought his words to others. I contrasted my perception of Lousiville: cuisine of fresh salmon, hominy grits with smoked gouda cheese and fine bourbon; nightlife so populated guards issue wristbands and check ID's just to enter the downtown area with Merton's perception:

> ***In Louisville, at the corner of Fourth and Walnut, in the center of the shopping district, I was suddenly overwhelmed with the realization that I loved all those people, that they were mine and I was theirs, that we could not be alien to one another even though we were total strangers.*** – Thomas Merton as cited by James Martin, SJ, *Becoming Who You Are*

Spiritual lens led me to see downtown differently, as I viewed others' inherent desire to be good. Divine acceptance of others. Merton's precision reaches within my soul to describe the experience of my own awakening. Thomas Merton once wrote, "The heart is an organ of knowing, affirming what we already know in our contemplative self. *We have been given everything we need*, because we know reconciliation of spirit and the transformation of taking it to others."

We Seek Reconciliation

Noticing our inner strength and profound wisdom calls us to create a counterculture of compassion. We destroy or reject realities, systems, and establishments culturally created from fear (even religious establishments), and create systems of compassion. Letting go is always our power of choice through mindful discernment and stages of interior freedom and growth. Without inner freedom, we remain in our suffering. Despair and fear are always broken spiritedness, and we heal from within rather than shallow external fixes and medications. We take time to reconcile our inner conflict.

> ***Despair is, ultimately, a form of pride that chooses misery instead of accepting the mysterious designs of God's plans and acknowledging that we are not capable of fulfilling our destinies by ourselves. Despair places our own limited perspective above God's.*** – Merton, *New Seeds of Contemplation*

We listen to our despair and suffering in order to move into growth and transformation, experiential learning and memories of *knowing*. Ironically, it is often our gifts that interconnect with our suffering. The gift of my hypersensitivity brings me the beauty of intuiting sensual beauty in writers like Anais Nin, and musical genius in Crosby, Stills, Nash and Young, Stephen Tyler, Outkast and numerous others. Further, the gift of my hypersensitivity brings me the mystical connection of spirit that lovingly is my heartfelt passion and joy. Conversely, the suffering of my hypersensitivity creates the chemical food allergies, and foggy periods as reminders of my necessary healing. A lens of understanding for my *gift* of being allows me to transcend the difficulties of my health as temporary and necessary *suffering*. But I came to this only after transformation in suffering. Divine seems distant in despair, a process known as "dark night of the soul", challenging us to seek clarity of intimacy. As created beings we create the necessary awareness to see a next step of growth. We practice being fully present to divine intention.

Dark Night of the Soul

Plummeting economy and housing market became my recent "dark night of the soul", my chaos of wondering where our God was, and my opportunity to see differently. My intuition knew there was a spiritual lesson for my husband and I together in the suffering. In the desert of my experience, I searched my heart to discover the lesson as if I could speed up the process by fixing it with my personal relationship with God sooner. I fell victim to the internal dissonance of needing control rather than letting go in trust. Serendipitously, our priest spoke on the "dark night of the soul" one Sunday. I turned to my husband, "You know, there is something in this house business we have yet to learn – it's about moving into a deeper place of trust with God or it's about us with each other." I *knew* this and we discussed and discerned what that might mean. The discussion brought me to a space where I could let go and trust. The following day we received the answer: a showing from our realtor and a serendipitous meeting with a flower woman. It's easy to follow spiritual path during times of noticing and nudging and being spiritually led, but we also grow in the patience of waiting out the desert of our chaos and confusion. I *knew* from unique perspective of a desert experience what it would look like if my God were giving me just what I needed in just the right way. And when I received exactly what I needed in just the right way, I celebrated in gratitude.

We move into sacred space and sense a fleeting glimpse of truth. I recently learned a deeper trust amidst financial insecurity when our house did not sell before our relocation, and we were making double house payments for a few months – and needing to trust we had everything we needed amidst the experience. Later, I saw God providing. One month, we received an insurance kickback just as the house payment was due. Another time, my contract settled and I received backpay, again, just before a house payment deadline. We were given everything we needed.

So I celebrated the financial gain when we sold the house, but I was really celebrating a deeper gift of knowing, listening, and walking the mandorla of my experience which allowed me to intimately *know* the experience as it transpired in God's time. I celebrate with loving color surrounding me in my new home: lime green flowers with lavender accent and black, dramatic background; jeweled valances and silk pillows; creations and mixes of eclectic pieces I treasured from past with retro, trendy new. Each morning I sit on the stairwell and drink hazelnut flavored coffee and view mochas and caramels accented with nuances of butter yellow and serene teal.

I *knew* we were selling the house when I bought cut flowers. As the woman and I discussed preferences of yellow daffodils amidst peach tiger lilies and bright oranges of sunflowers competing with sunshine yellows, I remarked I needed to choose quickly because I still needed to clean for a showing of our house. She looked at me with kind gray/blue eyes and a gentle smile of understanding as she spoke, "You'll sell the house with these flowers. It's happened twice now." I left carrying flowers and carrying much less burden in my heart. I believed her. I released and let go. I *knew.*

I was transformed through the suffering of my soul just as present culture can learn transformation amidst suffering. Mathew Fox, formerly of the Roman Catholic Church, applies "dark night of the soul" to present society. He leads us to radical transformation in an article entitled "Holy Impatience." Fox reminds us of potential energy created in the "bottoming out" experience of suffering. He says, "I think what is happening right now is a dark night of the soul and a dark night of our species. The question is, can we tap into that moral outrage?" (p. 22). Indeed, we can. We ought tap into our souls and bring about the healing of a generation. Reverend Matthew Fox is calling for a radical transformation. He discusses a national experience of "dark night of the soul" amidst the chaos after the attacks of 9/11. Fox speaks of authentic healing of spirit:

> ***The deeper response to chaos comes out of the mystical tradition for dealing with the dark night of the soul. First you do purification, and then you find out what it is you really cherish and what you are really longing for.***
>
> – Matthew Fox, "Holy Impatience"

Contemplative presence brings us to our purity each and every time. Clarity is purity and truth. Fox speaks of the same vision of interconnectedness as other contemplative mystics. We listen to process of purity in order to achieve our own blessed mysticism. In doing so, we rise to the gift of our being and a community of rising into a "radical transformation" of change. Our goodness prevails as we cherish our Selves and we Cherish Sophia. Sophia savors nudgings and gentle, loving movement as the base of power that can produce a radical transformation in connected lens of compassion and active spiritual voice.

Reconciliation: Gift of Clarity and Resolution of Conflict

We purify ourselves to be empty and let go of all. Emptiness allows us to be filled only with energy and spirit to be taken to other. A non-denominational understanding of reconciliation is defined in an article by Erik Doxtader, a communication theorist, as cited in the *Quarterly Journal of Speech*. "Reconciliation – A Rhetorical Conception" distinguishes human need to begin anew, whole. He cites Hegel, a young philosopher:

> ***Opposition is the possibility of reunification, and the extent to which in affliction life is felt as an opposite is also the extent of the possibility of resuming it again. It is in the fact that even the enemy is felt as life that there lies the possibility of reconciling fate. ... This sensing of life, a sensing which finds itself again, is love, and in love fate is reconciled*** – Hegel, *The Spirit of Christianity*)

Hegel resonates the Beat notion of being weary, or "undramatically pushed up against the wall of oneself." Opposition provides opportunity for our souls to transcend. We cherish Sophia and listen in order to empty ourselves of the chaos and confusion. Complacency and confusion of clashing needs are barriers to moving ahead in desire to heal, to remain whole, to guide others to wholeness. Sophia responds – we mindfully notice.

As long as humans have existed, there's been need to reconcile or purify. Herein lies wholeness. Doxtader discusses the Greek need for reconciliation in 400 BCE to move away from violence and conflict and into change. Reconciliation included "feasts, trials, pardon, oaths, prayers, arbitration, negotiation, contract, and purchase" (p. 270). The transformation from violence or negative experience into positive, possibly loving experience fulfilled a need for literal survival. We, too, reconcile and survive when we choose to view a situation differently, with a new lens, in order to magnificently survive and rise. We place the boundaries of our relationships and life experience to maintain our spiritual health. Beatniks removed boundaries with acid-based experiences. We open up in spirit and remove boundaries, as well, in order to *know* where to *meaningfully* place boundaries of reconciliation: in our relationships and life experiences. Boundaries create the line of how things *ought* to be as we gently protect, maintain, and build interconnected power. Reconciliation is also purity of *knowing* response to *become someone more in life situations.*

We ought to celebrate diverse perspective as potential to enhance the richness of life experience. Again, we move into our heart knowledge and limitless healing, through individual nuance and noticing of reconciliation. We reconcile when we open up and view anew, and the definition is broad, beautiful, and breathtaking. Wordless experiences that lack clear language are usually filled with remarkable silence and unspeakable bliss. We let go of the need to even name or define mystical experiences intended uniquely for us to savor. When we forgive and are forgiven, we experience opportunities of reconciliation. Reconciliation rests as a feather on those who accept forgiveness. The horrors of the Apartheid situation moving through the process of Reconciliation taught the world a process of global healing--wholeness rather than division. Savored resolution of conflict. Desmond Tutu urged, "Without forgiveness, there is no future."

A Sacrament of Reconciliation

All paths of reconciliation lead to opening up, to healing. Reverent personal experience is diverse, blissfilled, and "growing edge" as we step into the risk of the unknowing, the next step of our spiritual path amidst human experience, savoring heartfelt experience, lavished love and forgiveness/acceptance. Enjoy unique experiences of reconciliation. Many religious communities provide opportunity and process for Sacrament of Reconciliation. I did not experience the sacrament of individual Roman Catholic formal Reconciliation until two years ago.

The need for Reconciliation with Christian God is created from sin and weakness. Remorse for the action can create feelings of guilt that move an individual even further from God. There is a need to bring individuals back to intimate, personal relationship. Baptism is reconciliation, but adult choice to re-establish this, or open up to God, comes through the Sacrament. According to the Sacrament of Penance and scripture:

> ***because of human weakness, Christians 'turn aside from [their] early love' (cf. Rv. 2:4) and even break off their friendship with God by sinning. The Lord, therefore, instituted a special sacrament of penance for the pardon of sins committed after baptism (cf. Jn. 20: 21-23), and the Church has faithfully celebrated it throughout the centuries – in varying ways, but retaining its essential elements*** – *Catholic Encyclopedia*

My priest listened to me tell transgressions against loving self and others and responded in prayer and forgiveness. I remember noticing the forgiving and being surprised at the force of the lifting, loving, and forgiving. I can't define the experience further, nor do I feel the need to … it defies description in its holiness.

The point simply and beautifully is to move into our individual interpretation of reconciling with self/others/divine whenever and however we need. Individual reconciliation births the passion to create reconciliation with others and on a global scale. Viewing social problems with a religious lens is currently creating division. We are called to view world problems with a lens of spiritual presence and social justice and interconnectedness. We all are mindfully called to action – to be agents of change in world of need. We are called to transcend complacent living. New lenses are catalysts for world change. Reconciliation, indeed, brings purity and mystical moments of *knowing* we are exactly where we are intended to be.

The Calling: a Counterculture of Compassion

Cherishing feminine spirit and Sophia wisdom, we embrace diversity – especially where religious communities divide. Similarity exists … we need only pay attention from our sacred space. Diverse learning is the richness of life experience. We blend the connectedness of Eastern meditation and Western prayerfulness with the authority of feminine voice and create a counterculture of compassion – a global embracing and owning of compassion … a means of creating Heaven on Earth. Matthew Fox calls us to notice this time of radical healing and transformation:

> ***Buddhism is explicit about compassion, for example, although I think that the Jewish and therefore Christian traditions are more explicit about justice – but justice is a part of compassion. The Western prophets bring a kind of moral outrage, what I call a holy impatience, whereas the East brings a serenity and an emphasis on patience. I think there's a time for both, but I think we are in a time now of holy impatience.*** – Matthew Fox, *Holy Impatience: An Interview with Matthew Fox,* by Sarah Ruth van Gelder

I know truth of interconnectedness with Fox, Doxtader, Tutu and numerous other writers and artists, the many souls connected to my intuitive knowing. We are called into becoming the artists of our most precious creations: presenting beauty and love to others in our individual gifted form. We are called to heal the separation of cultures, conflict, and violence. We needn't create barriers with language of definition of a concept or sacrament that moves us to unspeakable, unfathomable healing and bliss. We are called to vibrate our connectedness to all and move into a wholeness of feminine energy and nonviolence. Sr. Elaine Prevallet is a Sister of Loretto in Sante Fe. She speaks of our wholeness, citing Merton: "Contain all divided words in self and transcend them in Christ." Transcendence is healing and wholeness.

I am mystically connected to a truth beyond Sr. Elaine's words – a calling of interconnectedness and unconditional, loving possibility for transformation and Heaven on Earth. Awakened souls respond.

Sr. Elaine believes we've intentionally evolved to the current opportunity. She points out the sufferings of the sixties and seventies that transformed our society to know the compassion and experience of Eastern mindful meditation combined with Western prayerful practice. Society embraced a myriad of opportunities: breath, mantra, yoga, transcendental meditation, Buddhism, and concern for the ecology. Recent years have birthed an embracing of mystical quality with compassion and experiential knowing. In fact, spiritual direction and contemplative listening moved out of heirarchical religious establishments and became popular with laity in the 1970's. What if we are exactly where we need to be at exactly the right time to respond to a magnificent healing? What if it's our place to listen in sacred space and rise to sacred places of interconnection, and global reconciliation? We've been presented with a gift of calling and limitless possibility; a Global Opportunity to resurrect our earth and its souls amidst present suffering. We are called to act with compassion toward ecological, political and social justice systems. In rising to our calling, we interconnect on a global, spiritual scale toward healing. We mystically embrace Holy Spirit as it integrates all religions, in our lifetime. Sophia God is feminine reality of hope and compassion. We cherish opportunity of knowing every breath and action affects the energy of a universe. We align our energies in prayer and meditation. Intuitively we know a time of uncertainty brings us to a letting go of need for certainty in order to look to our greatest gift of healing: our countenance. We rise in Confidence and Authority and Power.

Cherish Sophia to recognize individual stirrings and nudgings within. We cast off conventional values of our upbringing to fully embrace conventional and Post-conventional experience vision of our deepest embraces and ownership of being. Stirred passion catapults souls into places of divine intent … and we extraordinarily belong. We fit. Created beings create new possibility.

We take our gift to others in created forms and loving energy. We find verbal messages to convey experiences that transcend and defy description. We engage in nonverbal displays of countenance and actions that resonate just what those in the experience of our human experience need most. We *intend* to forgive, love, heal. Discernment brings us to true nature, even our cellular connections. We resonate our truth with others, and we are attractive in our countenance of Hope. Christiane Northrup, M.D. speaks of ultimate vibrations of Hope:

> ***know that when you are tuned into your heart, your Inner Wisdom, and God, then your energy lightens up and your vibration literally changes. You become a beacon of light and peace. You become an uplifter and a peacemaker."***
>
> ***Imagine possibility. Imagine your sacred place in leading possibility.***

What do our souls vibrate to others? We literally connect with positive vibrations of hope. Hope-filled healing is when we feel we cannot bear one more breath as our heart is suffering, yet we reach deep within to pull out a flicker of our soul's flame. The precious spark illuminates a pain, remorse, or void and fills it with love that magnificently vibrates out to others. Energy fields of compassion surround physicality with a countenance: a luminous energy of love expanding to others. We vibrate differently. We walk in a mandorla, a universe of spirit and human experience holistically aware of the Hope we've become. Compassionate intent brings Heaven on Earth and Calm Abiding.

A Native American tale tells of an elder who said, "I feel as if I have two wolves fighting in my heart. One wolf is the vengeful, angry, violent one. The other wolf is the loving, compassionate one." The disciple asked, "But which wolf will win the fight in your heart?" and the elder responded, "It depends on which one I feed." (Chittister, p.103). Indeed, we choose to feed our transformation. We choose Hope to win in our hearts.

Hearts *know* we are heroic. We are called to notice opportunity. We are called to live heroically: interconnected beacons of feminine hope and leadership.

A View of Reconciliation: What it Looks Like

Reconciliation is an act of Spiritual Companioning. Remarkably, I now teach at the same university as my mentor, Bassey Eyo. We share an occasional "Epiphany lunch" and discuss the spirituality of teaching, writing, family and life place. The rhythm of friends eating warm shrimp salads, drinking cool ice teas, wiping mouths brings calm abiding and celebration of what we are able to give to students and to the world. He is genuinely complimentary and supportive of each and every student. He once told me, "Each student is a blessing. Each student comes to me in need of something. I am gifted with opportunity to provide for each and every situation." That is what a reconciled soul who openly connects to others looks like.

Social justice is a continuance of spiritual reconciliation. Current political systems and establishments have gone awry and we question intent. The Roman Catholic Church is undergoing social justice discussion and controversy of Vatican II beliefs with Pre-Vatican II beliefs. I cast off my religion to preciously find this place of unconditional love and belonging. It is our responsibility to search until we find deserving communities and/or religious establishments that act within authentic extensions of our own compassion and love. Further, it is my obligation to fight for Higher Good from within, from the sacred root of my goodness – especially as women are currently denied voice and power of decision-making. Sister souls are connecting in order to become agents of change vibrating equality of women amidst decision-makers of patriarchy. Prophetic voice, Joan Chittister, was asked why she remained in the Catholic Church.

> ***I realized that an oyster is an organism that defends itself by excreting a substance to protect itself against the sand of its spawning bed. The more sand in the oyster, the more chemical the oyster produces until finally, after layer upon layer of gel, the sand turns into a pearl. And the oyster itself becomes more valuable in the process. At that moment, I discovered the ministry of irritation.***
>
> – Joan D. Chittister, *New Designs: An Anthology of Spiritual Vision*

Wendy Sue-Altobell addresses the present status of women in a paper written for the St. John's University School of Theology in 2004. It is aptly named "As Grains of Sand: Voices of Today Speak About Gender Inequality." Sue-Altobell's words connect women throughout history who've "irritated" those in power and remained, even amidst inequality. Women's voices remain unheard:

> ***By and large, males continue to hold all of the powerful decision making roles. Women are minimized in liturgical roles since they are not allowed to celebrate any sacrament and rarely allowed to preside or preach at a liturgical function. Only recently has the Vatican ruled it acceptable to have girls serving as acolytes at Mass and women serving as lectors, although they cannot be formally installed as such. The arrangement of the lectionary and the prevalence of noninclusive language in scripture, prayers, and music continue to minimize and even ignore women in liturgies.***

Sue-Altobell encourages readers to look at all world major religions in terms of suffering from patriarchy. She states, "It is interesting that Catholic feminists seem to align themselves in a common struggle with feminist thinkers and activists of all religions" (p.10). A radical transformation of women's voice is currently being addressed by Sue-Altobell, Chittister, and numerous other important women who know Truth and Wisdom across our nation and in other origins. Women who've forgiven and reconciled are working to change the relationship of church establishment and women in a profoundly meaningful way, as intended by Christian text and Christ. The suffering extends to priests as well, as they travel among numerous parishes to provide sacraments and speak as vessels of guidance. Father Kevin Anderson, pastor of the Newman Center in St. Cloud:

> ***Granted there is a shortage of priests, yet when are we, the church, going to faithfully address the sinfulness of sexism that excludes women as equals in our leadership roles? I propose ordaining women as priests (or as a start, deacons) but not just as a 'solution' to a shortage problem. Ordained leadership is a right received from baptism for all people. Currently only one-half of our population is allowed to accept that right.***

Sue-Altobell cites women's passion to belong in the heirarchy of Catholic leadership: female recipients of Master of Divinity degrees increased 224% from 1977-1987, while male recipients only increased 4.6%. I applaud being part of a religious community that serves college students, and places boundaries where they ought to be. We are joined in reverent spirit to ancestors, mystics, and contemplative sacred souls who vibrate to us. We are not leaving. We are just getting started. That is what reconciliation looks like.

Father Kevin Anderson is used to getting into the "messy" part of Roman Catholicism. He likes the phrase "An injustice done to any one of us is an injustice to all of us." He used that phrase again in a homily just before his parish was "reported" to the Bishop in the summer of 2004 because a woman, Kathy Langer, was reading the Gospel lesson – the reporting was an injustice to women. He used the phrase in February of 2006 because of a statewide movement to create an amendment to the constitution concerning marriage – the amendment was an injustice. Specifically, the Bishops of Minnesota were sending cards to each parish in the state of Minnesota to support the amendment. Father Kevin refused to support it. He stated:

> ***Our constitution doesn't need an amendment; it already defines marriage as between a man and a woman. You'd have to be pretty naïve not to see this campaign as a direct affront to gay and lesbians, who have definitely become one of our newest groups of lepers.*** (from unpublished sermons)

He speaks of societal views toward gay population as a symbolic representation of leprosy because of the way we've marginalized the culture and denied rights of health benefits and recognition of union in a committed relationship. He speaks his Truth:

> ***The fact is ... that God created a certain number of people attracted to their own gender. If you have a problem with that, take it up with God not the Minnesota Constitution! Another fact is that a paradigm shift is occurring in our culture concerning gays and lesbians. And the more they continue to speak up, speak out and come out ... we can't ignore them, discriminate against them, withhold benefits and treat them like lepers.***

The amendment suggests a campaign strategy or attempt to get conservative and evangelical voters to the polls. Division rather than wholeness. Fear and judgement rather than Love and Understanding. I find it deplorable that those who claim to act toward Christian belief and scripture frequently forget Matthew 7:1 "Judge not that ye be not judged". It's all love, remember? Father Kevin guides college students and permanent members toward acts of social justice. Father Kevin is what healing of Reconciliation looks like.

Examination of individual reconciliation leads to the power of reconciliation in community with others. What does your Reconciliation look like? Live the Abundance of your Truth. Create Reconciliation and lead to Heaven on Earth.

I once heard Thomas Merton quoted as saying, "It's not what's happening to us, it's what we are going to do." We spend our lives coming to this. We *come* and we *become*. Compassion and Confidence replace fear and need to control. We are creating the counterculture of compassion each time we listen to our stirrings within. Indeed, we shed need to control destiny, and find our **True Confidence**.

> ***If there is a light in the soul, there will be beauty in the person. If there is beauty in the person, there will be harmony in the house. If there is harmony in the house, there will be order in the nation. If there is order in the nation, there will be peace in the world."*** – Chinese Proverb

> ***Women are on the front lines. Women have always been the first to see what is coming.*** – Sobonfu Somé

Chapter Thirteen

Celebration and Gratitude

Walk in such a way that peace becomes a reality in every cell of your body, in every cell of your consciousness, because our consciousness is also made of cells. Mental formations, feelings, perception – they're all in the cells of our consciousness. And when we breathe peacefully, the peace of our breath will penetrate into our body and into our mind. Then very soon, in no time at all, body, mind, and breath will become one in concentration, and we'll get the energy of stability, solidity, and freedom generated by every step we make.

– Thich Nhat Hanh, *Walking with Peace and Presence*

Sister Aggie gently touches the nape of my neck as she begins my massage. My body is immediately filled with warmth of knowing profound connection. She once told me she could sense an aura of such love surrounding my body, and I believe her because she affirms my truth. My gift is my unconditional love I offer and I send out and receive such ethereal love beginning in the moment she caresses my woman's voice and healing. A smell of rosemary, lavender, and lemongrass awakens my senses as she prays for my goodness, my healing, my guardian angels guidance, and my brother, Jesus Christ to bless my being. Aggie's flowing rhythm of oil and skilled caress massage my body into complete state of being: wholeness of physical, emotional, intellectual and spiritual weaving. An experience of *Beyond Rational.* A rooster crows, birds chirp and water ripples. Calming music and presence of spirits hold me and carry me to a place so familiar, so like home: it is the rebirthing of my inner child and spirit. I own this place and I lovingly embrace the mystical experiencing of divine presence. I cherish Sophia.

A string of pearls encircles a women's voice in wisdom. The pearls are life experience; connected but separate. The thread is the secure piece that interweaves to form the necklace, adorning in beauty. Indeed, the mystical form of our being is our only necessary thread of constancy--our certainty. The only things we know to be true are our mystical and ecstatic knowing. Life voice of being sure. This place is our wisdom and power. Mystical experiences of noticing divine penetrating our silence and daring to show us appropriate view of life experience creates the beads of beauty and inner joy. We are transformed by beads of integrated, experiential learning of such grand love. The fun of walking life's spiritual journey is the surprise of seeing the "aha" as mystical experiences and beads of our human experience suddenly relate to the string of connectedness: our love and compassion. I view my life from a place of eternal gratitude.

I am Catholic and exactly in the place I should be. Zane's experience with whales and nature is extended to the artistry and spirituality of his teaching; exactly where he should be. Authorship of spirituality communes with others in music, literature, and art – exactly where created beings should be. Spirituality in diverse extensions of religious choice brings souls to where they should be. If we are connected to inner spirit, we are exactly where we should be. We discover the only certainty and constancy there is … and we've moved into countenance and power of our being. I *know* I will continue to experience the divine: in spiritual direction work; in teaching; in literature, music, and art; and in relationship with others who view world from a similar lens. I am certain. I am sure.

Awaken and listen to your soul. As there is suffering in life, so is there grace. Awaken to an embracing and cherishing of acceptance and movement toward your definition and experience of God or Divine. Deeper wisdom shows us the way to reconcile self with self, others, and divine. We are filled. We are connected. All is right. Wrap your soul around the spirit of my message and create your own message of connectedness. You already have everything you need to live happily and meaningfully.

St. Therese of Licieux lived simply and lovingly. She prayed of the roses or graces in life path. Indeed, it is in silence we are able to feel hearts touched by divine spirit as gentle as petals of roses fragrantly touching, healing, showing us life path. We live with intent to notice the petals, to notice the roses in silence. My words are blessed and sent to you through St. Therese who prayed for us to receive showers of roses – and we do. Open up and *Cherish Sophia*, the Sacred Feminine.

St. Theresa's Prayer

May today there be peace within.

May you trust God that You are exactly
where you are meant to be.

May you not Forget the infinite possibilities
that are born of faith.

May you use those gifts that you have received,
and pass on the love that has been given to you.

May you be content knowing you are a child of God.

Let this presence settle into your bones, and allow your soul the
freedom to sing, dance, praise and love.
It is there for each and every one of us.

May you see your holiness.

Acknowledgements

I live my life fully awake as the result of gifts of those around me: my students, my guides and mentors, my friends, and my family. No one person ever truly writes a book. Rather, it is the culmination of what is meant to be as experienced by an individual. I live in deepest gratitude for all students who've touched me in some manner and become a part of me. I am especially grateful to those who never knew they would shape the words and message of this book. Far more students have marked my life than could ever be expressed in words – all have shaped my heart, head and soul and I remember them dearly.

Kelly Isaacson wears a tattoo on her foot that reads, "Carpe Diem". I laughed aloud when I first saw it, because I'd already consulted with her as my "mentor student" to make sure of the clarity of my message with college age group. Kelly is going great places and I can't wait to see her next path unfold. She lives life fully aware of her passion and power. She and I "seize the day", watching for opportunities to celebrate and enjoy. We live life fully aware and create opportunities for other women to know.

Stefanie Weisgram, O.S.B. from St. Benedict Monastery gave me tears when she believed I could write words worthy of her editing. Joanna Pucell is a kindred soul and treasured colleague who guided the intent of my words: spoken and written. I am fortunate, indeed with heartfelt support.

Kathy Langer, Pastoral Associate continues to shape messages in my heart that become the thinking and attitudes of my transformation. Kathy lives her authentic form and leads with such an intent, as an angel who graces others with her work. Kevin Anderson shapes messages in my head that become heartfelt knowing and walking as they extend into my physical form. Kevin Anderson is the man who helped discover my feminine voice. I'm deeply transformed because I know great leaders who teach me to embrace unconditional love of self, others, and establishment.

Kathy's prayers are heartfelt Knowing of Divine. Kevin's prayers breathe God into my soul. I am blessed.

Cherish wholeness. Cherish Sophia.

Suggestions for Listening

Kelly Isaacson's recommendations for experiential listening:

"Video"—India Arie

"Somewhere Over the Rainbow"—Israel Kamakawiwo'ole

"Boston"—Augustana

"Banana Pancakes"—Jack Johnson

"Soul Meets Body"—Death Cab for Cutie

"Fix You"--Coldplay

"Fighter"—Christina Aguilera

"Undeniable"—Mat Kearny

"Breathe"—Anna Nalik

"Mudfootball"—Jack Johnson

"Come Clean"—Hilary Duff

"Cowboy Take Me Away"—Dixie Chicks

"Breakdown"—Jack Johnson

"Dream Big"—Ryan Schupe

"Sinner"—Neil Finn

"Superman"—"Scrubs" soundtrack

"Rent"—musical soundtrack

"What's Up"—Four Non-Blondes

"Paradise"—Joni Mitchell

"You're My Little Girl"—Go Fish

"Island in the Sun"--Weezer

Works Cited

Adler, Ronald B. and Rodman, George. *Understanding Human Communication* (Ninth Edition). New York: Oxford, 2006.

Adler, Ronald B. and Towne, Neil. *Looking Out Looking In* (Eighth Edition). Fort Worth: Harcourt Brace, 1996.

Anderson, Fr. Kevin and Nate Mathews. "Longing for God", *Longings*. Tatar Studios: St. Joseph. 2001.

Barker, Eileen. "What the BLEEP Does Spirituality Have to Do with Conflict Resolution?" *ACResolution: The Quarterly Magazine of the Association for Conflict Resolution*, (Fall 2005): 10, 11.

Bowling, Daniel. "Who Am I as a Mediator? Mindfulness, Reflection and Presence". *ACResolution: The Quarterly Magazine of the Association for Conflict Resolution*, (Fall 2005): 12-14.

Broderick, Robert C., ed. *The Catholic Encyclopedia*. Nashville: Thomas Nelson, Inc. 1987.

Campbell, Karlyn Kohrs. *The Rhetorical Act* (Second Edition). Belmont: Wadsworth, 1996.

Cantor, Joanne, Ph. D. *Mommy, I'm Scared: How TV and Movies Frighten Children and What We Can Do to Protect Them.* Orlando: Harcourt Brace, 1998.

Chittister, Joan D. O.S.B. *New Designs: An Anthology of Spiritual Vision.* Erie: Benetvision, 2002.

Chittister, Joan D., O.S.B. *Scarred by Struggle, Transformed by Hope*. Grand Rapids: Eerdman, 2003.

Conroy, Maureen, R.S.M. *Looking into the Well: Supervision of Spiritual Directors.* Chicago: Loyola, 1995.

Cooley, C.H. *Human Nature and the Social Order*. New York: Charles Scribner's Sons, 1902.

Covey, Stephen R. *Seven Habits of Highly Effective People: Powerful Lesson in Personal Change*. New York: Simon and Schuster, 1989.

Douty, Linda. "Hearing the Silence" in *Reflections for Your Journey,* June 15, 2005.

Doxtader, Erik. "Reconciliation – A Rhetorical Concept/ion." *Quarterly Journal of Speech* 89, (November 2003): 267-292.

Durand, Leo H. *The Psychology of Happiness.* Blackstone: Merit Press, 1968.

Fincham, Frank D. "The Kiss of the Porcupines: From Attributing Responsibility to Forgiving." *Personal Relationships* 7 (2000), 1-23.

Finn, Myrna, Ed.D. "Communicating From Wholeness." Presented at the National Communication Association Conference, 2003.

Fowler, James W. *Stages of Faith: The Psychology of Human Development.* New York: HarperCollins, 1981.

Fox, Matthew. *Original Blessing*. New York: Putnam, 1983.

Glenn, Cheryl. *Unspoken: A Rhetoric of Silence*. Carbondale: Southern Illinois University, 2004.

Goffman, E. *The Presentation of Self in Everyday Life* (Garden City, Ny: Doubleday, 1959), and *Relations in Public* (New York: Basic Books, 1971).

Goleman, Dan. *Emotional Intelligence*. New York: Bantam, 1995.

Haber, Rabbi Yaacov. "ELUL: A Time to Reflect", based on "Tomer Devorah" class, February 2006.

Hart, Hilary. *The Unknown She: Eight Faces of an Emerging Consciousness.* Inverness: The Golden Sufi Center, 2003.

Hoagland, Tony. "Grammar". *Donkey Gospel.* Graywolf Press: Pittsburgh, 1998.

Lama, His Holiness, The Dalai. *How to Practice: The Way to a Meaningful Life*. New York: Pocket Books, 2002.

Lampman, Lisa Barnes, and Shattuck, Michelle D., eds. *God and the Victim: Theological Reflections on Evil, Victimization, Justice, and Forgiveness.* Grand Rapids: Eerdmans Publishing, 1999.

Lawrence, Gary. *The State of Faith.* Minneapolis: Kirkhouse Publishers, 2002.

Luhrman, Baz. "Everybody is Free to Wear Sunscreen." *Something for Everybody.* Australia: EMI Music, 1997.

Maltz, D.N., & Borker, R. "A Cultural Approach to Male-female Miscommunication." In J.J. Gumpertz (Ed.), *Language and Social Identity* (pp. 196-216). Cambridge, UK: Cambridge University Press.

Martin, James, SJ. *Becoming Who You Are: Insights on the True Self from Thomas Merton and Other Saints.* Mahwah: Paulist Press, 2006.

Matthews, Gray, Ph.D. "Thomas Merton and a Contemplative Foundation for the *Practice of Communication". Presented at the Convention of the National* Communication Association, 2004.

May, Gerald. *Addiction & Grace: Love and Spirituality in the Healing of Addictions.* New York: HarperCollins, 1988.

Merton, Thomas. *A Year with Thomas Merton: Daily Meditations from His Journals.* New York: HarperCollins, 2005.

Merton, Thomas. *The Inner Experience: Notes on Contemplation.* New York: HarperCollins, 2003.

Merton, Thomas. *The Wisdom of the Desert.* Gethsemane: The Abbey of Gethsemane, Inc., 1960.

Metts, Sandra, Ph.D. "Face and facework: Implications for the Study of Personal Relationships". In S. Duck (ed.), *Handbook of Personal Relationships: Theory, Research, and Interventions* (second edition) (373-390). New York: Wiley, 1997.

Myss, Caroline. *Sacred Contracts: Awakening Your Divine Potential.* New York: Three Rivers Press, 2003.

Nin, Anais. *The Novel of the Future.* Athens: Swallow Press, 1986.

Northrup, Christianne, M.D. "Some Thoughts on Peace". Handout.

Obbard, Elizabeth Ruth. *Medieval Women Mystics: Gertrude the great, Angela of Foligno, Birgitta of Sweden, Julian of Norwich: Selected Spiritual Writings.* Hyde Park: New City Press, 2002.

Piaget, J. *The Psychology of the Child.* New York: Basic Books, 1972.

Raugust, Dale L. "The Spiritual Aspects of Collaborative Law". *Mediate.com: Supporting Effective Agreement.* January 29, 2006.

Ritberger, Carol, Ph.D. *Your Personality, Your Health.* Carlsbad: Hay House, 1998.

Rohr, Richard. *Adam's Return: The Five Promises of Male Initiation.* New York: Crossroad, 2004.

Rolheiser, Ronald. *The Holy Longing: The Search for a Christian Spirituality.* New York: Doubleday, 1999.

Sheldrake, Philip. *Spirituality and Theology: Christian Living and the Doctrine of God.* Maryknoll: Orbis Books, 1999.

Smedes, Lewis B. *The Art of Forgiving: When you Need to Forgive and Don't Know How.* New York: Ballantine, 1996.

Sue-Altobell, Wendy. "As Grains of Sand: Voices of Today Speak About Gender Inequality." St. John's University School of Theology, 2004.

Tannen, Deborah. *He said She Said Gender, Language & Communication.* Los Angelos: Into the Classroom Media, 2001.

"Thich Nhat Hanh". Plum Villaige. Mehrac, France.January 19, 2006.

Van Gelder, Sarah Ruth. "Holy Impatience." *Yes! A Journal of Positive Futures,* Winter 2006.

Weber, Christin Lore. *Blessings: A WomanChrist Reflection on the Beatitudes.* San Francisco: Harper & Row, 1989.

Wolvin, Andrew, and Coakley, Carolyn. *Listening* (Fifth Edition). Boston: McGraw Hill, 1996.

Wright, J. C., Kunkel, D., Pinon, M., & Huston, A.C. "How Children Reacted to Televised Coverage of the Space Shuttle Disaster". *Journal of Communication*, 39, 27-45.

"Forgiveness is a Call to Action". *A Course for Teachers* 1 June 1994: 1-8.

"Danger of Cults is Growing", **F**ight **A**gainst **C**oercive Tactics Network, Inc. June 2004: 1.